NEW DIRECTIONS FOR STUDENT SERVICES

Evolving Theoretical Perspectives on Students

Leila V. Moore
The Pennsylvania State University

EDITOR

Number 51, Fall 1990

JOSSEY-BASS INC., PUBLISHERS
San Francisco

12-20-93

EVOLVING THEORETICAL PERSPECTIVES ON STUDENTS
Leila V. Moore (ed.)
New Directions for Student Services, no. 51
Margaret J. Barr, Editor-in-Chief
M. Lee Upcraft, Associate Editor

LC 85-644751 ISSN 0164-7970 ISBN 1-55542-815-0

NEW DIRECTIONS FOR STUDENT SERVICES is part of The Jossey-Bass Higher Education Series and is published quarterly by Jossey-Bass Inc., Publishers (publication number USPS 449-070). Second-class postage paid at San Francisco, California, and at additional mailing offices. POSTMASTER: Send address changes to Jossey-Bass Inc., Publishers, 350 Sansome Street, San Francisco, California 94104.

EDITORIAL CORRESPONDENCE should be sent to the Editor-in-Chief, Margaret J. Barr, Sadler Hall, Texas Christian University, Fort Worth, Texas 76129.

Cover photograph by Wernher Krutein/PHOTOVAULT © 1990.

10% POST CONSUMER WASTE

The paper used in this journal is acid-free and meets the strictest guidelines in the United States for recycled paper (50 percent recycled waste, including 10 percent post-consumer waste). Manufactured in the United States of America.

CONTENTS

EDITOR'S NOTES

After it was published in 1978, *Applying New Developmental Findings* (New Directions for Student Services, no. 4) rapidly became one of the most sought-after volumes available to educators and student affairs practitioners. For educators, the book provided a clear explanation of what were then key developmental theories related to student affairs. It also served as a renewed rallying point for the central role that theory must play in our profession. For practitioners, the book updated the knowledge base of staff whose preparation did not include a basic education about our theoretical roots. Research and programs, based on theories examined in the volume, proliferated.

More than ten years have passed since the volume was published. Certain changes in the field have modified the utility of the book. The theories themselves have undergone a developmental process, in which some have been modified, others have diminished in viability and application, and still others have moved to positions of increased prominence. For the theories in current use, there is still a need to update both our understanding of the theories and our awareness of new research related to them. Finally, with increased attention to the diverse populations represented among today's students, researchers and theorists have turned to new models as a way to explain and predict the behaviors and attitudes of these student groups. Within the most recent proliferation of models is a growing clarity about the importance of understanding the ethnic and cultural backgrounds of the students and their families. This context is missing in our current understanding and use of developmental theory.

Evolving Theoretical Perspectives on Students will be useful to graduate faculty who seek current information about theory and research for their graduate courses. For practitioners seeking direction or justification for programs and services, this volume will provide a clear view of which theories or models have the greatest relevance to their particular programmatic concerns. But one limitation became apparent as the volume developed: space limitations would restrict the treatment of theories to outline descriptions, precluding full discussions. Although the purpose of this book is met by such cursory description of theories influencing the profession, those readers who require specialized depth of knowledge will have to supplement their readings. Three clusters of theory are especially affected by the space limitations of this book: counseling, career development, and person-environment interaction.

Chapter One of this volume is a review of the history of applied theory. In this chapter, Leila V. Moore and M. Lee Upcraft also introduce the next five chapters, which include perspectives on gender, age, sexual orientation, ethnicity, and cultural diversity. In Chapter Two, Linda Kuk's discussion of perspectives on gender differences includes an elaboration of the influence of Carol Gilligan and others on the shift away from a linear view of growth. In Chapter Three, LuAnn Krager, Robert Wrenn, and Joan Hirt review the models and theories pertaining to the adult learner in the student development literature. In Chapter Four, Nancy Evans and Heidi Levine discuss the identity development of gay, lesbian, and bisexual students. W. Terrell Jones reviews perspectives on ethnicity in Chapter Five, including the concept of Eurocentricity. His discussion of ethnocentric differences in values and views of the world provides a bridge to Chapter Six, where Paul Shang and Leila V. Moore place these various perspectives back into the context of the campus environment. Theories about the relationship of persons to environment are described here. The authors characterize the institutional climate as a critical mitigator of student growth and suggest new approaches to developing an inclusive multicultural value system within the institutional climate. The endnotes of this chapter introduce Robert D. Brown and Margaret J. Barr's final chapter, which is a focus on new roles for student affairs practitioner-theorists. Finally, the Appendix to this volume contains a bibliography of additional sources for further study of student development theory.

Leila V. Moore
Editor

Leila V. Moore is with the Division of Student Programs at The Pennsylvania State University, University Park. She is also president-elect of the American College Personnel Association.

The authors trace the history of student development theory and then review theories that are now in use or emerging.

Theory in Student Affairs: Evolving Perspectives

Leila V. Moore, M. Lee Upcraft

The student affairs profession has always used theoretical perspectives about students to guide its practice. Our original theory of student development, in loco parentis, served us for more than three hundred years. Since 1960, our theories, as reflected in the writings of our scholars and reported in our journals, have been clarified, tested, and modified. In the 1980s, we have become increasingly conscious of the inadequacies of and gaps in our theories. For example, African-American student development is not adequately explained by theories based on white students. Gender differences are not adequately explained by theories based on male students. Only recently have we seen the emergence of models and theories that address these and other inadequacies of our traditional student development theories. In this chapter we clarify the terminology used in discussing theory, review the history of student development theory, and orient the reader to the other chapters of this volume.

Definition of Terms

Too often when discussing student development theory, we interchange the terms "theory" and "model." Theories, according to Harmon (1978, p. 36), "are sets of definitions and statements specifying the relationship between the defined concepts." Theories have three functions: they explain phenomena, they predict outcomes, and they permit us to influence outcomes. Theories are usually based first on multiple observations of the same phenomenon under different circumstances. These observations become the foundation of beliefs about why and how that phenomenon occurs. The beliefs are then tested through application in other settings and evolve into theories to be tested and refined further.

As the student affairs profession developed over the years, practitioners and researchers "tried on" a variety of theories from personality theory to system theory. We became aware that the most useful theories focused on human development and took into account the unique status and role expectations of college students. In 1972, Robert Brown attached the term "student development theory" to the subset of theories in his monograph *Student Development in Tomorrow's Higher Education: A Return to the Academy.*

As our attention over the past twenty years focused specifically on student development theory, the gaps became increasingly apparent. When there are no relevant theories to explain phenomena, theorists and researchers construct models (Marx, 1963). Models, like theories, explain the relationships between variables under examination. Unlike theories, they lack the specificity of clear definitions. Instead, they include analogies: this is like that observation, but not like this observation. Theory emerges as these analogies become definitions. Models are, in effect, emerging theories. With refinement and further testing, these models evolve theories.

The First Student Development Theory: In Loco Parentis

The first student development theory used by institutions of higher education was based on the principle of in loco parentis. The early colonial colleges believed they had a responsibility to act on behalf of parents for the good of their students. Students were considered children, and the institution their "parents." In fact, the average age of seventeenth-century freshmen was about fourteen, so there was some legitimacy to treating them as children.

So much has been made of in loco parentis as the legal relationship between students and their institutions that we forget that it originally had a developmental rationale: the development of Christian moral character. In fact, historian Frederick Rudolph argues that the development of students' character was substantially more important than the development of their intellect. For example, President Lord of Dartmouth once said, "The very cultivation of the mind has frequently a tendency to impair the moral sensibilities . . . of students." President Talbot of Dennison agreed: "At college we tend to exaggerate the importance of the intellect." But mostly, the college experience was moralistic, theistic, and rationalistic, and not seen in conflict with intellectual pursuits. When there was a conflict, morality and theology prevailed (Rudolph, 1962).

This original student development theory was applied through a highly controlled and contained environment governed by extensive rules, strictly enforced by the president and the faculty. Rules were very specific and rigidly enforced. Punishments were severe and often included floggings, suspension, and expulsion (Rudolph, 1962). The dimensions of Christian moral character were very well defined, the factors influencing that character were known, and the purpose of higher education, to develop a Christian moral character, was unchallenged by any other authority. In spite of the emergence of the social sciences in the late nineteenth century, and the development of counseling theories in the first half of the twentieth century, the development of Christian moral character was the predominant developmental theory that guided the college careers of students until the mid-twentieth century.

Twentieth-Century Influences

The first secular influence on our thinking about college students emerged in the late nineteenth century, when psychological theorists such as Freud and Jung began to write about humans from a perspective different from that of theologians and philosophers. As the field of psychology developed, theorists such as B. F. Skinner influenced the student affairs profession. Undoubtedly, the most influential psychologist in this regard was Carl Rogers. For many student affairs professionals trained in the 1950s and 1960s, before the emergence of what we now call student development theory, Rogers (1951, 1961) provided a very powerful theoretical basis for our work. His "client centered" theory of counseling was a combination of assumptions based on self-psychology, phenomenology, and self-actualization principles. His concept of "unconditional positive regard," in which the counselor maintained a nonjudgmental attitude toward the client, was adopted by many student affairs practitioners as the central principle of interpersonal relations.

Initially, however, psychological theorists focused on adults, and it was only later that psychologists such as Erik Erikson began to focus on adolescent development. Erikson (1950, 1968) was the first to look at personality development in a social context and to define the identity development of youth. His often-quoted (and frequently misunderstood) concept of identity crisis has become an accepted part of our thinking about student development. Erikson believed that the task of establishing one's identity is especially critical during the college years, during which time youth must redefine themselves. This period of development can be a time of emotional turmoil, or even of massive personality disorientation.

Another influential psychologist was Jean Piaget (1964). Although Piaget is primarily known as a child development theorist, two aspects of his work have particular relevance to student development. The first is his notion that mental structures gradually become more complex through the process of problem solving and analysis. The second is his description of equilibrium and disequilibrium. When current mental structures fail to be useful in problem-solving activities, a period of confusion, discomfort, or disequilibrium occurs. In this confused and sometimes painful state, the person begins the process of restoring equilibrium by developing more complex mental processes. Students may be seen as moving from simple to more complex mental processes, and through equilibrium/disequilibrium stages.

The second secular influence on student affairs theory emerged in the early twentieth century. This was the vocational guidance movement, initiated by Frank Parsons in 1909. In the book *Choosing a Vocation,* he described the activities involved in choosing an occupation. This early description advanced the theory of matching self-understanding (interests, abilities, and opportunities) with the requirements of a particular occupation. Over the next forty years, vocational guidance turned on this match principle. The "best fit" was the outcome sought, and research in this area focused on assessment of interests and abilities. Over the next fifty years the need for additional theory grew stronger as more college graduates focused on the goals of personal happiness and self-satisfaction in their search for meaningful employment. By the 1950s, work had emerged as a primary source of life satisfaction insofar as it rapidly became the "organizing focus for one's identity" (Tyler, 1969, p. 132).

Theories of career development proliferated during the 1950s and early 1960s. Notable among this group of theorists was Donald Super (1957), who hypothesized that career choice includes continuous updating of knowledge about self and knowledge about the world of work. Super's work was followed by that of several other theorists who added to our understanding of decision making, life planning, the special considerations of returning adults in career choice, vocational development, and vocational maturity.

John Holland (1966) developed a personality typology that investigated the determinants of occupational choice. He identified six distinct personality types: realistic, intellectual, social, conventional, enterprising, and artistic. He then related these types to a classification of corresponding model environments to produce his theory of vocational choice. "For Holland, the typology described both students and subcultures (environments) and the theory predicts that students of a given type will choose an occupation located in an environment matching that type" (Katchadourian and Boli, 1985, p. 40).

The third major influence on theory was the development of the student personnel profession, beginning with the appointment of Thomas Arkle Clark as the first dean of men at the University of Illinois in 1909. The landmark publication *Student Personnel Point of View* of the American Council on Education (1937), while not a student development theory, did offer some basic assumptions about how students grow and develop in the collegiate environment. They include the following:

- Intellectual development is just one aspect of the growth of a student; other aspects include social, emotional, interpersonal, moral, and vocational development.

- Theories about college students are not meant to be used to treat all students as though they had the same characteristics. These theories describe the relationships between and among different characteristics.
- The education process is interactive, not linear.
- The education process involves not only knowledge but also skills and attitudes.

Later, writers such as Gilbert Wrenn (1951), Esther Lloyd-Jones and M. R. Smith (1954), Kate Hevner Mueller (1961), and E. G. Williamson (1961) began to focus on college students and higher education as a legitimate field of study.

Student Development Theory in the Mid-Twentieth Century

Our assumptions about students and their development suffered a serious challenge with the popularization of a college education. Up until World War II, college was really for the elite, upperclass male. Only about 10 percent of high school graduates actually went on to college. The first significant expansion and diversification of the college student population came just after World War II, when veterans attended colleges in droves as a result of the first federal financial aid effort, the GI Bill. These veterans, who had fought all over the world for their country, had little tolerance for the rigid rules by which colleges attempted to regulate their lives. They were the first to challenge in loco parentis as a practical basis for defining the relationship between students and their institutions. They were not to be the last.

Psychological Theories. In the early 1960s, for the first time, social scientists began to theorize more specifically about college students. During this period, theories emerged about how students grow and change, what aspects of growth most affect college students, what clusters of personality types and college environments are represented in American higher education, and what sources from the campus environment most often influence growth and change.

Nevit Sanford's *American College* (1962) contained many postulates about students that are still relevant today. For example, he believed that student development is expressed in terms of the concepts of *differentiation* and *integration.* Students learn about themselves by identifying various personality characteristics within themselves and understanding how these characteristics shape their respective identities as unique human beings. Sanford (1967) later postulated the concepts of support and challenge. He argued that students attempt to reduce the tension or challenge of the collegiate environment by striving to restore "equilibrium." The extent to which students are successful at this task depends on the degree of *support* that exists in the collegiate environment. Too much challenge is overwhelming; too much support is debilitating. The challenge-support cycle results in growth and change. Sanford's writings were followed by Arthur Chickering's (1969) *Education and Identity*. He expanded Sanford's concepts of integration and differentiation to include what he called seven "vectors of development," discussed later in this chapter.

Also during the late 1960s and early 1970s personality typology theorists began to focus on college students. For example, Roy Heath (1964) described the college male as the "reasonable adventurer"; Clark and Trow (1966) analyzed various student subcultures, including academics, nonconformists, collegiates, and vocationals; Peter Madison (1969) postulated a student development theory based on psychoanalytic concepts; Douglas Heath (1968) combined five developmental trends that define maturation with four structures that define the person; and Florence Brawer (1973) developed the concept of functional autonomy. In the mid-1970s, Jane Loevinger's (1976) concepts about ego development provided particularly useful ways of understanding relationships between ego development and interpersonal interaction, approaches to individual life situations or problems, and cognitive style. She defined eight growth stages in ego development that closely parallel the work of Erikson and other psychological theorists.

Theories of Reasoning and Cognitive Development. In the 1970s, another trend in theory emerged. Other theorists, instead of developing generalized theories of student development, began to look at specific aspects of student development. For example, William Perry (1970) developed a theory of intellectual and ethical development in which students moved in nine stages from a simplistic, categorical view of the world to a more relativistic, committed view. According to Perry, freshmen start out with an unquestioning, dualistic framework of conceptions (right-wrong, good-bad, beautiful-ugly) and grow to the realization of the contingent nature of knowledge values and truth. As they move through the nine stages of development, they integrate their intellects with their identities, gaining a better understanding of the world and finding personal meaning in it through an affirmation of their own commitments. Patricia King (1978) summarized Perry's nine stages in the following four clusters:

1. *Dualism (stages 1–2).* Students in this stage view people, knowledge, and values through absolute, discrete, and concrete categories. "Right answers" are determined by established authorities, and students learn simple truths without substantiation and without question. Alternative perspectives or multiple points of view are confusing and thus not acknowledged. Truth is self-evident.

2. *Multiplicity (stages 3–4).* Students acknowledge multiple points of view, but they still feel that questions simply have multiple answers. All points of view are equally valid and thus not subject to judgment. The questioning or challenging of viewpoints is still avoided. Toward the end

of this stage, students begin to distinguish between an unconsidered belief and a considered judgment. Authorities tend to be defied or resisted.

3. *Relativism (stages 5–6).* Students believe knowledge is contextual and relative. Multiple points of view are now seen as pieces that fit together into a larger whole. Students who seek the big picture are able to analyze and evaluate their own ideas as well as those of others. Authorities are valued for their expertise, not their infallibility. Often relativism results in indecision because to make a judgment would sacrifice appreciation for another's view. Toward the end of this stage, however, students begin to endorse their own choices from the multiple "truths" that exist in a relativistic world.

4. *Commitment in relativism (stages 7–9).* Students in this stage (if they get this far) have made an active affirmation of themselves and their responsibilities in a pluralistic world, establishing their identities in the process. Personal commitments in such areas as marriage, career, or religion are formulated from a relativistic frame of reference. Identities and life-styles are established in a manner consistent with students' personal themes.

Similarly, Lawrence Kohlberg (1971) developed a cognitive stage theory of the development of moral judgment. Although he did not develop his theory exclusively for college students, his ideas are often applied to student development. In his view, moral judgment is a progression through various stages of development, each stage representing a mode or structure of thought. He is concerned about how and why judgments are made, as opposed to their content. The structure of moral thought includes the decision-making system, the problem-solving strategy, the social perspective, and the underlying logic in making a moral choice. Alexander Smith (1978) consolidated Kohlberg's six stages of moral development into three groups:

1. *Preconventional level (stages 1–2).* "At this level the child is responsive to cultural rules and labels of good and bad, right and wrong, but interprets these labels either in terms of the physical consequences of action (punishment, reward, exchange of favors) or in terms of the physical power of those who enunciate the rules and labels" (Smith, 1978, p. 55). In stage 1 (punishment and obedience orientation), the physical consequences of an action determine its goodness or badness; in stage 2 (instrumental-relativist orientation), right action is that which satisfies one's own needs and occasionally the needs of others.

2. *Conventional level (stages 3–4).* "At this level maintaining the expectations of the individual's family, group, or nation is perceived as valuable in its own right, regardless of immediate and obvious consequences. This attitude is not only one of conformity to personal expectations and social order, but of loyalty to it, of actively maintaining, supporting, and mystifying the order, and of identifying with the persons or group involved in it" (Smith, 1978, p. 55). In stage 3 (interpersonal concordance orientation), behavior is evaluated by whether other persons approve or disapprove and by inten-

tion. One earns the approval of others by being "nice." In stage 4 (law-and-order orientation), good behavior consists of doing one's duty, showing respect for authority, and maintaining the given order for its own sake.

3. *Preconventional, autonomous, or principled level (stages 5–6)*. "At this level, there is a clear effort to define moral values and principles that have validity and application apart from the authority of groups or persons holding these principles and apart from the individual's own identification with these groups" (Smith, 1978, p. 56). In stage 5 (social contract, legalistic orientation, generally with utilitarian overtones), right action is defined for general individual rights, based on standards examined and agreed on by society. Relativism of personal values is accepted. Procedural rules for reaching consensus are established, based on laws and the Constitution. Outside the legal realm, free agreement and contract are the binding elements of obligation.

Sociological Theories. Psychology was not the only discipline to affect our thinking about students. Also in the late 1960s, several sociologists argued that to have a complete understanding of college student development, one has to look not only at the students but also at the environments in which they live. They focused on the interpersonal aspect of the campus environment, with a special emphasis on the powerful influence of the peer group. The first notions about peer group influence were articulated by Newcomb and Wilson (1966) when they introduced the idea of the peer group's powerful effects on students in the first six weeks of college. Feldman and Newcomb (1969) summarized the peer group influence in more specific terms: (1) help students achieve independence from home and family, (2) support or impede the institution's academic goals, (3) offer students general emotional support and fulfill needs not met by the curriculum, classroom, or faculty, (4) give students practice in getting along with people, particularly those whose backgrounds, interests, and orientations differ from their own, (5) provide students support for changing, or not changing, and (6) affect staying in or leaving college.

The general study of student environments then expanded beyond the peer group to the more generalized concept of campus ecology. In the mid-1970s we began to look at the influence of campus environments on student development, focusing on the relationship between the student and his or her environment. Several theorists contributed to the ecological perspective, including Barker's (1968) behavioral-setting theory, Clark and Trow's (1966) subculture approach, Holland's (1973) personality types and model environments, Stern's (1970) need-press culture theory, and Pervin's (1968) transaction model. Readers who want more detailed information about these theories should consult Walsh (1978).

In 1973 the Western Interstate Commission for Higher Education outlined some basic assumptions of the ecological perspective based on these theories and research about college students:

1. Students enter college with their own personalities, attitudes, values, skills, and needs, based on their prior experiences in their homes, families, communities, and peer groups.
2. Students enter into an environment never before encountered; physically different from anything experienced before, more homogeneous and intense.
3. The collegiate environment can have a powerful impact on students, depending on its history, composition, size, collective attitudes, values, and needs.
4. Students, particularly freshmen, have a great need to identify and affiliate with other students, and campus facilities, faculty, staff, and students provide this opportunity.
5. Students affect environments, and environments affect students.
6. Some students are very susceptible to the press of the environment, while others seem immune.
7. Some environments are weak, unstable, and rapidly changing, while others are strong, stable, and less likely to change.
8. When there is congruence between the student and his or her environment, the student is happier, better adjusted, and more likely to achieve personal and educational goals.
9. Collegiate environments can be described, influenced, and channeled by the institution for the betterment of students.

These basic assumptions were reinforced by the research of Astin (1973) and Chickering (1974), both of whom confirmed the powerful influence of the residential environment. They found that freshmen who live in collegiate residence halls, compared to those who live elsewhere, are more likely to earn higher grades, stay in college and graduate, and experience more positive personal development.

Student Development Theory in the 1980s

In the 1980s, we diverted our attention from the psychological and social foundations of theory established in the two preceding decades to work on the task of "filling in the theoretical gaps" left behind by earlier researchers. However, with the increased social and cultural diversity of students over the course of those two decades, the 1980s also brought serious challenges to existing student development theories, because those theories failed to fully explain the development of student subpopulations, such as women, racial and ethnic groups, older students, international students, homosexual and bisexual students, student athletes, honors students, and commuters. Models of student development specifically geared toward these groups proliferated in the 1980s, tapping the theoretical and methodological resources of other fields of study, such as medicine, theology, and anthropology. In Chapter Six, Paul Shang and Leila V. Moore discuss the interaction of increasingly diverse student populations with their collegiate environments.

Current General Theories of Student Development

The late 1980s brought continued exploration of specific aspects of student development, including spirituality, values, learning styles, ethics and decision making, family backgrounds and dynamics, life experiences prior to college, "mattering," and involvement.

Involvement Theory. Currently, the most often quoted student development theory is Alexander Astin's (1985) involvement theory. Basing his theory on the extensive body of retention literature, Astin believes that students learn best in the collegiate setting by becoming involved, that is, by investing physical and psychological energy in the academic experience. His involvement theory comprises five basic postulates:

1. Involvement refers to the investment of physical and psychological energy in various "objects." The objects may be highly generalized (the student experience) or highly specific (preparing for a chemistry exam).

2. Regardless of its object, involvement occurs along a continuum. Different students manifest different degrees of involvement in a given object, and the same student manifests different degrees of involvement in different objects at different times.

3. Involvement has both quantitative and qualitative features. The extent of a student's involvement in academic work can be measured quantitatively (the number of hours the student spends studying) and qualitatively (the student reviews and comprehends reading assignments, or he or she simply stares at the textbook and daydreams).

4. The amount of student learning and personal development associated with any educational program is directly proportional to the quality and quantity of student involvement in that program.

5. The effectiveness of any educational policy or practice is directly related to the capacity of that policy or practice to increase student involvement.

Mattering/Marginality Theory. According to Schlossberg, Lynch, and Chickering (1989), student success is dependent on the degree to which students feel they "matter." "Mattering" refers to the beliefs people have, justifiably or not, that they matter to someone else, that they are the objects of someone else's attention, care, and appreciation. In the collegiate environment, students must believe that they matter and that others (peers, faculty, staff, and family) care about them. They must have a sense of belonging if they are to succeed. They must feel appreciated for who they are and what they do, if they are to grow, develop, and succeed in college. If students feel "out of things," ignored by the "mainstream," and unaccepted, they will feel marginal and are therefore much less likely to succeed in college. Minority students in predominantly white institutions are often most susceptible to these feelings of marginality.

Freshman Development. Another general approach to student development is Vincent Tinto's (1987) theory of freshman development. Tinto reflects on the stages of freshman integration into college life and suggests that by extension, the process of student departure can be conceptualized as three distinct stages: separation, transition, and incorporation.

In the separation stage, freshmen disassociate themselves from membership in past communities, homes, schools, and work places. For students just out of high school, this means breaking away from family and reaching closure on relationships with high school friends. Separation begins during the last year of high school as going off to college is anticipated. New students in the separation stage reject the values of family and community in order to adopt those values perceived as appropriate to college life.

The transition stage bridges the old and the new. New students have not yet acquired the norms or established the personal bonds needed for full integration into the college community. When the differences between the old and the new are extreme, freshmen will probably encounter more difficulties in learning the new norms, values, and behaviors. For example, the transition can be expected to be more difficult for ethnic minorities, older adults, and those from very poor and/or rural backgrounds.

To successfully negotiate the incorporation stage, freshmen must establish full membership in both the social and academic communities of college life. Social interactions are the primary vehicle through which such integrative associations occur. Individuals need to establish contact with other members of the institution, students and faculty alike. Failure to do so may lead to dropping out. Experiences important to freshman success in this stage include participation in orientation seminars, good peer support, knowledge of student and academic services, and at least one caring relationship with a faculty or staff member.

Chickering Revisited. The work of Arthur Chickering has been consistently among the most widely applied theories of student development. Since 1969, with a substantial base of research to support his theory, Chickering has made some adjustments to his original seven vectors (Thomas and Chickering, 1984). If he were to revise his vectors today, he would add or change the following:

1. *Developing competence.* This vector was originally defined as students' ability to develop intellectual competence, physical and manual skills, and social and interpersonal competence. With respect to intellectual competence, Chickering would take into account recent advances in what is known about reflective thought, brain dominance, and learning theory. With respect to physical and manual skills, he would take into account our

more complete understanding of nutrition, exercise, and other wellness concepts. With respect to interpersonal competence, he would include the interpersonal competencies needed for the world of work, including the skills of active listening, constructive feedback, and public speaking.

2. *Managing emotions.* This vector was originally defined as students' ability to manage the key emotions of aggression and sex, and to broaden their range of emotions. Chickering saw an increased urgency for management of emotions because of the increase in campus violence, substance abuse, date rape, and sexual harassment. He would add anxiety and depression as other emotions to be managed because of an increase in prolonged depression, suicide gestures, and completed suicides among students.

3. *Developing autonomy.* This vector was originally defined as students' ability to become emotionally and instrumentally independent, primarily from parents and peer groups. Today Chickering would change this vector to "developing interdependence," or moving from individualism to greater emphasis on social responsibility and global interdependence. He would recognize interdependence as the capstone of development.

4. *Establishing identity.* This vector was originally defined as students' ability to develop a sense of self by clarifying physical needs, characteristics, and personal appearance through establishment of appropriate sexual identification, roles, and behaviors. Chickering would add recent concepts about gender role development, including sexual orientation, and would dissolve age norms linked to career and family.

5. *Freeing interpersonal relationships.* This vector was originally defined as students' ability to develop an increased tolerance for others, a capacity for intimacy, and relationships based on trust, independence, and individuality. Chickering would now place greater emphasis on the importance of developing high levels of tolerance and acceptance because of increasing cultural pluralism in America, and increasing global interdependence. He would recognize the changing conditions under which one learns about intimacy, since marriage is now not the only context for sustained intimate relationships. And he would focus on students learning more about single parenthood, dual-career couples, couples living together but not married, and homosexual couples.

6. *Clarifying purposes.* This vector was originally defined as students' ability to develop a sense of purpose in their lives, leading to plans and priorities for careers, avocations, and life-styles. Chickering would now move from the assumption of "one life, one job pattern" to a multiple-career perspective. He acknowledges that stress in the workplace makes the risk of integration of family, leisure, and work more difficult. Work in service of the self seems to be ascending over work in service of others.

7. *Developing integrity.* This vector was originally defined as students' ability to develop a personally valid set of beliefs that has internal consistency and provides a guide for behavior. Chickering now includes devel-

opment of a sense of social as well as personal responsibility. He believes we must educate students about environmental pollution, toxic wastes, exploitation of the powerless, and the increasing gap between the haves and the have-nots. He believes knowledge implies a responsibility to act.

Specialized Theories of Student Development

Spiritual Development. Some critics have argued that most developmental theories are exclusively secular and ignore students' spiritual development. Theorists such as Westerhoff (1976) and Parks (1986) have written about the spiritual development of young adults. Fowler (1981, 1987) proposes six stages of faith development, which help us understand the spiritual development of college students:

Stage 1: intuitive-projective faith (early childhood). Fantasy and limitation are powerful influences in young children, who are not yet capable of logical thinking. Thus, children are profoundly influenced by the moods, actions, and language of the adults around them. As conceptual thinking emerges, children become concerned with knowing the nature of things and the difference between what is real and what only appears to be real.

Stage 2: mythic-literal faith (childhood and beyond). Persons in this stage adopt the stories, beliefs, and observances that symbolize being part of a community. Moral rules, attitudes, and beliefs are interpreted literally. If individuals perceive that stories contradict each other, literalism breaks down, and the conflicts between authoritative stories must be faced. Mutual interpersonal perspective-taking emerges.

Stage 3: synthetic-conventional faith (adolescence and beyond). The world now extends beyond the immediate family. New cognitive abilities allow for mutual perspective taking. Faith must now provide a basis for one's personal identity and outlook as well as synthesize personal and family-based values and information. Transition to the next stage can occur only when there are serious contradictions between valued authority sources, marked changes in practices previously deemed sacred and immutable, and challenges made by the individual who is able to see the world from a relativistic point of view.

Stage 4: intuitive-reflective faith (young adulthood and beyond). Individuals at this stage recognize the need to take responsibility for their commitments, life-styles, beliefs, and attitudes. Certain tensions emerge, such as individuality versus definition by group membership, self-fulfillment versus service to others, relativity versus absoluteness in viewpoint. Transition to the next stage can occur when disturbing inner voices and disillusionment with one's compromises direct the individual toward a multidimensional approach to life and truth.

Stage 5: conjunctive faith (mid-life and beyond). Individuals at this stage are open to the voices of their deeper selves. They come to recognize the prejudices, ideal images, and myths that are part of self-esteem by virtue of one's experiences, social class, religious tradition, or ethnic group. In this stage individuals strive to unify opposites in mind and experience. Transition to the next stage can occur when individuals become increasingly uncomfortable living and acting in the in-between state of an untransformed world and their transforming visions of the ultimate environment.

Stage 6: universalizing faith (mid-life and beyond). In this stage, people move beyond paradoxes and polarities and become grounded in a oneness with the power of being, or, more specifically, a sovereign god. Their visions and commitments free them for a passionate yet detached spending of the self in love, devoted to overcoming division, oppression, and brutality. People in this stage include Gandhi, Martin Luther King, Jr., and Mother Teresa.

Cognitive Development. Another domain of theory that has been historically neglected by student development theorists and practitioners is cognitive development. Perhaps that is because student affairs practitioners tend to see their role as involving the psychosocial development of students outside the classroom as opposed to the cognitive development of students inside the classroom. Nevertheless, cognitive development is important and should be included in our base of student development theory.

David Kolb (1984) believes learning is a cycle. He has developed a four-stage model of learning, including reflective observation, abstract conceptualization, concrete experience, and active experimentation. By Kolb's account, a learner enters the learning cycle at a stage determined by his or her own habits and preferences, but in order for learning to take place, the learner must pass through all four stages, perhaps several times, and not necessarily in the same order each time.

The reflective observation stage involves understanding ideas from different points of view and forming opinions from the process of taking in many different ideas. The abstract conceptualization stage involves looking at the logic of an idea and systematically using ideas or theories to solve problems. This is the thinking stage of learning. The other two stages, concrete experience and active experimentation, involve, respectively, learning from one's feelings and from one's actions. In the concrete experience stage, learning includes personal involvement in daily situations and experiences. In the active experimentation stage, one learns by solving real problems and carrying out real projects.

Student Development and Persons of Color

Student development theorists have been criticized for not fully explaining the development of persons of color. Most critics acknowledge that students of color are in many ways similar to other students in their development. However, these same critics argue that existing developmental theories make certain assumptions about the commonality of environments, cultures, and backgrounds of students that simply are not valid. They also argue that being raised in a minority culture amidst a majority society creates different developmental outcomes for youth of that culture. Parental roles, child-rearing practices, cultural values, community commitments and obligations, and other culture-related factors combine to produce different developmental dynamics for minority students. Many developmental theories assume that culture-related factors are constant and ignore cultural differences in explaining minority students. But these cultural differences are too pronounced to be ignored (Wright, 1987).

In Chapter Five, W. Terrell Jones presents several theories that focus on persons of color and cultural identity, including W. E. Cross (1978), Helms (1984), Vontress (1981), Sue and Sue (1971), Atkinson, Morten, and Sue (1983), Asante (1988), Martinez (1988), and Johnson and Lashley (1988).

Student Development and Gender

Carol Gilligan's (1982) landmark work *In a Different Voice* argues that contemporary theories of human development fail to take into account possible differences in male and female development. She believes that Freud, Erikson, Piaget, Kohlberg, and others mistakenly based their concepts of human development on male behavior and, in the process, totally misrepresented female development. For Gilligan, the concepts of *autonomy* and *separation* are indicative of male development, and female development is better explained by the concepts of *connectedness* and *relationships*. She believes that Erickson's fifth stage (youth) stresses separateness rather than connectedness, "with the result that development itself comes to be identified with separation, and attachments appear to be development impediments, as is repeatedly the case in the assessment of women" (Gilligan, 1982, pp. 12–13).

Gilligan also believes that Kohlberg's theory mistakenly portrays women as deficient in moral development, because his stage-3 factors of helping and pleasing others are not ends in themselves but rather necessary steps on the way to higher stages where relationships are subordinated to rules (stage 4), and rules to universal principles of justice (stages 5 and 6). She believes that advanced stages of moral development for women may well include their care for and sensitivity to the needs of others, and that Kohlberg's later stages should include the concept of connectedness so as to make his theory valid for women.

In Chapter Two, Linda Kuk discusses Gilligan's work in greater depth, as well as other theories, including Belenky, Clinchy, Goldberger, and Tarule (1986), Josselson (1987), O'Neil and Roberts Carroll (1988), and Downing and Roush (1985).

Student Development and Adult Learners

Patricia Cross (1981), in her landmark publication *Adults as Learners,* was one of the first to challenge the age bias of student development theories. She interpreted adult student development in the light of adult developmental learning theories, including force field analysis (Miller, 1967), expectancy-valence paradigm (Rubenson, 1977), congruence model (Boshier, 1973), and anticipated benefits theory (Tough, 1979).

Cross developed a "chain of response" model of adult learning in which adults start with self-evaluations that lead them to desire more education, if their prior experiences with education were positive. They establish appropriate goals and expectations that may be based on life transitions, either gradual in nature or related to sudden traumatic events such as loss of a job, divorce, or the death of a friend or family member. They then gather information about learning activities, special opportunities, and overcoming barriers. Finally, they participate in some learning activity.

Schlossberg, Lynch, and Chickering (1989) view adult learning as a transition process, which extends from the first moment one thinks about returning to college to the time when the experience is complete and integrated into one's life. They break down the transition process for adult learners into three main parts: moving into the learning environment, moving through it, and moving on or preparing to leave. For adult learners, the transition process may extend over many years, compared to eighteen- to twenty-one-year-olds. Also, the larger the transition, the more it pervades an individual's life.

In Chapter Three, LuAnn Krager, Robert Wrenn, and Joan Hirt discuss these and other theories about adult learners.

Student Development and Sexual Orientation

Until recently, gay, lesbian, and bisexual development was almost totally ignored by developmental theorists. While gay, lesbian, and bisexual students have a great deal in common with their heterosexual colleagues, they are faced with somewhat different developmental issues, based on their sexual orientation.

Cass (1979, 1984) identifies six stages of homosexual identity formation, which are differentiated on the basis of an individual's perceptions of his or her own behavior in relation to self-recognition as a homosexual, including identity confusion, identity comparison, identity tolerance, identity acceptance, identity pride, and identity synthesis. In Chapter Four, Nancy Evans and Heidi Levine analyze in greater depth Cass's theory, as well as other theories that help us better understand the development of gay, lesbian, and bisexual students.

Summary

In summary, the last thirty years have yielded five basic clusters of theories and models about college students. The first cluster, theories and models about personal growth and development, focuses on the genesis of student development. Theorists in the cluster include Erikson (identity development, 1968), Sanford (integration and differentiation, 1962), Chickering (vectors of development, 1969, [Thomas and Chickering] 1984), Loevinger (ego development, 1976), D. Heath (stages of maturation, 1968), Brawer (functional autonomy, 1973), Holland (career-choice personality typologies, 1966), Super (career choice, 1957), and Fowler (spiritual development, 1981).

The second cluster focuses on the way we think, make meaning, and reason. Theorists in this cluster include Perry (intellectual development, 1970), Piaget (complexity of mental structures, 1964), Kohlberg (moral development, 1971), Kolb (learning styles, 1984), King and Kitchener (reflective judgment, 1985), and Gilligan (connectedness and relationships, 1982).

The third cluster involves what we know about growing and changing. This cluster examines the many ways in which change occurs and is rich in suggestions for strategies of change. Theorists include Piaget (equilibrium/disequilibrium, 1964), Sanford (support and challenge, 1962), Gilligan (nonlinearity, 1982), Schlossberg, Lynch, and Chickering (mattering, 1989), Astin (involvement, 1985), and Tinto (transitions, 1987).

The fourth cluster includes theories and models about campus environments. Theorists here include Banning (campus ecology, 1978), various person-environment theorists mentioned previously, and Feldman and Newcomb (peer group influence, 1969).

The final cluster helps us understand how various aspects of a student's identity development are influenced by culture, race, ethnicity, gender, age, and sexual orientation. Theorists here include Cass (homosexual identity formation, 1979), Downing and Roush (feminist identity development, 1985), W. E. Cross (black identity development, 1978), Asante (Afrocentrism, 1988), Kluckhohn and Strodtbeck (cultural values, 1961), P. K. Cross (adult students, 1981), Scott (North American Indian culture, 1986), Martinez (Mexican-American culture, 1988), Padilla and DeSnyder (Hispanic students, 1985), and Sue and Sue (Asian-Americans and Pacific Islanders, 1985).

There is no doubt that as we now enter the 1990s, student affairs professionals will have an even greater responsibility to know and understand student development theories, given the increased diversity of American college students and of the collegiate environments in which they develop. We can no longer rely on one or two theories to guide our work. We must not only familiarize ourselves with emerging theory but also contribute to that theory base through our literature and research. This volume is intended to bring the practitioner up to date on existing theory and to show how theory can be useful in developing services and programs that maximize student development. Some of these theories are discussed in detail in this volume; others, however, are given only cursory treatment because of space limitations. Readers are advised to refer to original sources for in-depth analyses, and to refer to the bibliography provided in the Appendix.

References

American Council on Education. *The Student Personnel Point of View.* Washington, D.C.: American Council on Education, 1937.

Asante, M. K. *Afrocentricity.* Trenton, N.J.: Africa World Press, 1988.

Astin, A. W. "The Impact of Dormitory Living on Students." *Educational Record,* 1973, *54,* 204–210.

Astin, A. W. *Achieving Educational Excellence: A Critical Assessment of Priorities and Practice in Higher Education.* San Francisco: Jossey-Bass, 1985.

Atkinson, D. R., Morten, G., and Sue, D. W. *Counseling American Minorities: A Cross-Cultural Perspective.* (2nd ed.) Dubuque, Iowa: Brown, 1983.

Banning, J. H. (ed.). *Campus Ecology: A Perspective for Student Affairs.* Portland, Oreg.: National Association of Student Personnel Administrators, 1978.

Barker, R. G. *Ecological Psychology: Concepts and Methods for Studying the Environment.* Stanford, Calif.: Stanford University Press, 1968.

Belenky, M. F., Clinchy, B. M., Goldberger, N. R., and Tarule, J. M. *Women's Ways of Knowing: The Development of Self, Voice, and Mind.* New York: Basic Books, 1986.

Boshier, R. "Educational Participation and Dropout: A Theoretical Model." *Adult Education,* 1973, *23* (4), 255–282.

Brawer, F. *New Perspectives on Personality Development in College Students.* San Francisco: Jossey-Bass, 1973.

Brown, R. D. *Student Development in Tomorrow's Higher Education: A Return to the Academy.* Student Personnel Monograph, no. 16. Washington, D.C.: American College Personnel Association, 1972.

Cass, V. C. "Homosexual Identity Formation: A Theoretical Model." *Journal of Homosexuality,* 1979, *4,* 219–235.

Cass, V. C. "Homosexual Identity Formation: Testing a Theoretical Model." *Journal of Sex Research,* 1984, *20,* 143–167.

Chickering, A. W. *Education and Identity.* San Francisco: Jossey-Bass, 1969.

Chickering, A. W. *Commuting Versus Resident Students: Overcoming the Educational Inequities of Living Off Campus.* San Francisco: Jossey-Bass, 1974.

Clark, B. R., and Trow, M. "The Organizational Context." In T. M. Newcomb and E. K. Wilson (eds.), *College Peer Groups: Problems and Prospects for Research.* Chicago: Aldine, 1966.

Cross, P. K. *Adults as Learners.* San Francisco: Jossey-Bass, 1981.

Cross, W. E., Jr. "The Thomas and Cross Models of Psychological Negrescence: A Review." *Journal of Black Psychology,* 1978, *5,* 13–31.

Downing, N. E., and Roush, K. L. "From Passive Acceptance to Active Commitment: A Model of Feminist Identity Development for Women." *Counseling Psychologist,* 1985, *13* (4), 695–709.

Erikson, E. H. *Childhood and Society.* New York: Norton, 1950.

Erikson, E. H. *Identity: Youth and Crisis.* New York: Norton, 1968.

Feldman, K. A., and Newcomb, T. M. *The Impact of College on Students.* 2 vols. San Francisco: Jossey-Bass, 1969.

Fowler, J. W. *Stages in Faith: The Psychology of Human Development and the Quest for Meaning.* San Francisco: Harper & Row, 1981.

Fowler, J. W. *Faith Development and Pastoral Care.* Philadelphia: Fortress Press, 1987.

Gilligan, C. *In a Different Voice.* Cambridge, Mass.: Harvard University Press, 1982.

Harmon, L. W. "The Counselor as Consumer of Research." In L. Goldman (ed.), *Research Methods for Counselors.* New York: Wiley, 1978.

Heath, D. *Growing Up in College.* San Francisco: Jossey-Bass, 1968.

Heath, R. *The Reasonable Adventurer.* Pittsburgh, Pa.: University of Pittsburgh Press, 1964.

Helms, J. E. "Toward a Theoretical Explanation of the Effects of Race on Counseling: A Black and White Model." *Counseling Psychologist,* 1984, *12* (4), 153–164.

Holland, J. *The Psychology of Vocational Choice.* Waltham, Mass.: Blaisdell, 1966.

Holland, J. *Making Vocational Choices: A Theory of Careers.* Englewood Cliffs, N.J.: Prentice-Hall, 1973.

Johnson, M. E., and Lashley, K. H. "Influence of Native-Americans' Cultural Commitment on Preference for Counselor Ethnicity." *Journal of Multicultural Counseling and Development,* 1988, *17* (30), 115–122.

Josselson, R. *Finding Herself: Pathways to Identity Development in Women.* San Francisco: Jossey-Bass, 1987.

Katchadourian, H. A., and Boli, J. *Careerism and Intellectualism Among College Students: Patterns of Academic and Career Choice in the Undergraduate Years.* San Francisco: Jossey-Bass, 1985.

King, P. M. "William Perry's Theory of Intellectual and Ethical Development." In L. Knefelkamp, C. Widick, and C. A. Parker (eds.), *Applying New Developmental Findings.* New Directions for Student Services, no. 4. San Francisco: Jossey-Bass, 1978.

King, P. M., and Kitchener, K. S. "Reflective Judgment Theory and Research: Insights into the Process of Knowing in the College Years." Paper presented at the annual meeting of the American College Personnel Association, Boston, March 1985.

Kluckhohn, F. R., and Strodtbeck, F. L. *Variations in Value Orientations.* New York: Harper & Row, 1961.

Kohlberg, L. "Stages of Moral Development." In C. M. Beck, B. S. Crittenden, and E. V. Sullivan (eds.), *Moral Education.* Toronto: University of Toronto Press, 1971.

Kolb, D. *Experiential Learning: Experience as the Source of Learning and Development.* Englewood Cliffs, N.J.: Prentice-Hall, 1984.

Lloyd-Jones, E. L., and Smith, M. R. *Student Personnel Work as Deeper Teaching.* New York: Harper & Row, 1954.

Loevinger, J. *Ego Development: Conceptions and Theories.* San Francisco: Jossey-Bass, 1976.

Madison, P. *Personality Development in College.* Reading, Mass.: Addison-Wesley, 1969.

Martinez, C. "Mexican Americans." In L. Comas-Diaz and E.E.H. Griffith (eds.), *Cross-Cultural Mental Health.* New York: Wiley, 1988.

Marx, M. H. *Theories in Contemporary Psychology.* New York: Macmillan, 1963.

Miller, H. L. *Participation of Adults in Education: A Force Field Analysis.* Boston: Center for the Study of Liberal Education for Adults, Boston University, 1967.

Mueller, K. H. *Student Personnel Work in Higher Education.* Boston: Houghton Mifflin, 1961.

Newcomb, T. M., and Wilson, E. K. (eds.). *College Peer Groups: Problems and Prospects for Research.* Chicago: Aldine, 1966.

O'Neil, J. M., and Roberts Carroll, M. "A Gender Role Workshop Focused on Sexism, Gender Role Conflict, and Gender Role Journey." *Journal of Counseling and Development,* 1988, *67,* 193–197.

Padilla, A. M., and DeSnyder, N. S. "Counseling Hispanics: Strategies for Effective Intervention." In P. Pederson (ed.), *Handbook of Cross-Cultural Counseling and Therapy.* Westport, Conn.: Greenwood Press, 1985.

Parks, S. *The Critical Years: Young Adult Search for Faith to Live By.* San Francisco: Harper & Row, 1986.

Parsons, F. *Choosing a Vocation.* Boston: Houghton-Mifflin, 1909.

Perry, W. G. *Forms of Intellectual and Ethical Development in College.* New York: Holt, Rinehart & Winston, 1970.

Pervin, L. A. "Performance and Satisfaction as a Function of Individual-Environment Fit." *Psychological Bulletin,* 1968, *69,* 56–68.

Piaget, J. *Judgment and Reasoning in the Child.* Patterson, N.J.: Littlefield Adams, 1964.

Rogers, C. *Client-Centered Therapy: Its Current Practice, Implications, and Theory.* Boston: Houghton Mifflin, 1951.

Rogers, C. *On Becoming a Person.* Boston: Houghton Mifflin, 1961.

Rubenson, K. "Participation in Recurrent Education: A Research Review." Paper presented at the annual meeting of National Delegates on Developments in Recurrent Education, Paris, March 1977.

Rudolph, F. *The American College and University.* New York: Vintage Books, 1962.

Sanford, N. (ed.). *The American College.* New York: Wiley, 1962.

Sanford, N. *Where Colleges Fail.* San Francisco: Jossey-Bass, 1967.

Schlossberg, N. K., Lynch, A. Q., and Chickering, A. W. *Improving Higher Education Environments for Adults: Response Programs and Services from Entry to Departure.* San Francisco: Jossey-Bass, 1989.

Scott, W. J. "Attachment to Indian Culture and the 'Difficult Situation': A Study of American Indian College Students." *Youth and Society,* 1986, *17* (4), 381–395.

Smith, A. "Lawrence Kohlberg's Cognitive Stage Theory of the Development of Moral Judgment." In L. Knefelkamp, C. Widick, and C. A. Parker (eds.), *Applying New Developmental Findings.* New Directions for Student Services, no. 4. San Francisco: Jossey-Bass, 1978.

Stern, G. G. *People in Context.* New York: Wiley, 1970.

Sue, W. S., and Sue, D. W. "Chinese-American Personality and Mental Health." *Amerasia Journal,* 1971, *1,* 36–49.

Sue, W. S., and Sue, D. W. "Asian-Americans and Pacific Islanders." In P. Pedersen (ed.), *Handbook of Cross-Cultural Counseling and Therapy.* Westport, Conn.: Greenwood Press, 1985.

Super, D. E. *The Psychology of Careers.* New York: Harper & Row, 1957.

Thomas, R., and Chickering, A. W. "Education and Identity Revisited." *Journal of College Student Personnel,* 1984, *25,* 392-399.

Tinto, V. *Leaving College: Rethinking the Causes and Cures of Student Attrition.* Chicago: University of Chicago Press, 1987.

Tough, A. "Choosing to Learn." In G. M. Healy and W. L. Ziegler (eds.), *The Learning Stance: Essays in Celebration of Human Learning.* Final Report of Syracuse Research Corporation project. National Institute of Education, no. 400–78–0029. Washington, D.C.: National Institute of Education, 1979.

Tyler, L. *The Work of the Counselor.* (2nd ed.) New York: Appleton-Century-Crofts, 1969.

Vontress, C. E. "Racial Differences: Impediments to Rapport." *Journal of Counseling Psychology,* 1981, *18,* 7–13.

Walsh, W. B. "Person/Environment Interaction." In J. Banning (ed.), *Campus Ecology:*

A Perspective for Student Affairs. Cincinnati, Ohio: National Association of Student Personnel Administrators, 1978.

Westerhoff, J. *Will Our Children Have Faith?* New York: Seabury Press, 1976.

Western Interstate Commission for Higher Education. *The Ecosystem Model: Designing Campus Environments.* Boulder, Colo.: Western Interstate Commission for Higher Education, 1973.

Williamson, E. G. *Student Personnel Services in Colleges and Universities.* New York: McGraw-Hill, 1961.

Wrenn, G. *Student Personnel Work in Colleges and Universities.* New York: Ronald Press, 1951.

Wright, D. (ed.). *Responding to the Needs of Today's Minority Students.* New Directions for Student Services, no. 38. San Francisco: Jossey-Bass, 1987.

Leila V. Moore is with the Division of Student Programs at The Pennsylvania State University, University Park. She is also president-elect of the American College Personnel Association.

M. Lee Upcraft is assistant vice-president for Counseling and Health Services and affiliate associate professor of education at The Pennsylvania State University, University Park. He is also associate editor of New Directions for Student Services.

The justice and the care perspectives are two ideals of human relationships that serve as coordinates for viewing moral reasoning and moral emotion and that provide a realistic account of the observed similarities and differences in male and female behavior.

Perspectives on Gender Differences

Linda Kuk

Few would dispute the generalization that men have designed American higher education institutions for the purpose of educating young, affluent white males (Rich, 1975; Pearson, Shavlick, and Touchton, 1989). In this context, women's colleges emerged as structures modeled after male colleges, although more conducive to the development of women. The growth in the 1940s and 1950s of a national, coeducational focus in higher education still reflects the original standards of education for young, affluent white males. Even though women actually became the majority population on our campuses in the mid-1980s, they are still perceived and treated as a minority.

Recent reports indicate that campus environments are often hostile to women students and that women's success during college often occurs as a result of experiences and support gained outside of the college environment (Hall and Sandler, 1982; Pearson, Shavlick, and Touchton, 1989). It is not surprising that this "chilly" campus climate for women exists. Women's concerns and needs are not accommodated in the basic structure of our higher education institutions. Policies, procedures, and campus norms remain male-dominated. Even the foundations of our educational theory are built on a discipline of human development that in principles and in practices has excluded the study of women (Erikson, 1950; Piaget, 1952; Perry, 1970; Kohlberg, 1969).

The basic assumption that one could study white adolescent males and subsequently construct "human" development theory based on these studies has created numerous problems. First, it has misled educators into believing there is one "correct" educational model for all. Second, it has created considerable confusion and misdirection in exploring and understanding women's behavior and development. Third, it has perpetuated a serious research bias that undermines the validity of existing theory and hence challenges current educational practice.

This chapter begins the journey down those seemingly invisible paths of understanding that have been hidden from reality for so long that we have actually believed there is only one correct direction to follow. I explore here contemporary research on female development that highlights new directions of inquiry and provides new perspectives for understanding human development as well as student development theory and practice.

The presence of this new inquiry has seriously challenged the notion that a single-gender linear model of development is sufficient and accurate as a conceptual map of human development. Through continued, applied research on our campuses, these new insights can be used to shape new environments that support the development of all students regardless of gender, race, sexual orientation, or cultural background. How different would our understanding of human development be if women's experiences were included? How different would our campuses be if a more inclusive conceptualization of the developmental needs of women were key elements in the way we designed and administered our campuses? What effects would these constructs have on shaping the learning and development of women and men? How different would our world be if we celebrated diversity rather than expected all people to walk the same road?

The Evolution of "Human" Development Theory

Beginning with Freud's (1905) failure to fit women into his Oedipal theory and thereby his characterization of women as developmental failures ridden with envy, psychological theory has repeatedly depicted women's differences from men as deficient, sick, dysfunctional, or underdeveloped. Human developmental theorists consistently attempted to apply research findings and subsequent theories based on male subjects to the experiences and behavior of women, resulting in the portrayal of women as deviants.

Challenges to the single-gender, linear view began in the late 1970s. Prior to this time, psychological theory as well as student development theory focused on an expansion and description of what was believed to be a single-stage model of human development. Erikson (1950), Piaget (1952), Perry (1968), and Kohlberg (1969) are all examples of such single-stage models. For each of these theorists, growth from one stage to the next represented movement to more complex tasks, more complex understandings of self. During the 1970s a few feminist voices questioned the validity of this premise by suggesting the existence of other developmental models. Baker-Miller (1976, 1986), in her work with women in psychotherapy, theorized that a woman's sense of self is built around her ability to make and maintain relationships. Chodorow (1978), focusing on early stages of development, viewed the differentiating experiences in male and female development as arising from the fact that women are primarily responsible for early child care. That children begin life in a state of dependency, in most cases with the mother, leads to a primary identification with and attachment to the mother. Female children experience themselves as like their mothers and, as a result, fuse the experience of attachment with the development of identity. In contrast, male children see themselves as different from their mothers and find separation as the key to developing a masculine identity. In Chodorow's work, female development is viewed as normal and positive, yet different from male development.

From a more sociological perspective, Schaef (1981) presents the view that women's environments, cultures, and ways of dealing with the world are different from those of white men. She describes the environmental systems that create these socializing realities. Within the context of female development is a value system that treasures intimacy and the ethic of responsibility of caring for others and holds sacred the quality and continuation of relationships. She states that these environments are not gender specific but tend to be gender related, with women more likely to operate within the context of the "female" value system and men more likely to operate within the white "male" system that values separation and differentiation.

The Work of Carol Gilligan

Building on these early voices, Carol Gilligan (1982) successfully articulated the challenges to the traditional notions of developmental research and theory. An alternative model of human development emerged. Gilligan worked with Lawrence Kohlberg and others at Harvard University, investigating the topic of moral development. In her research, Gilligan uncovered data that seemed to support another approach to development. Through the voices of the women she interviewed, she unraveled a developmental pattern of dealing with moral dilemmas that did not fit into the traditional male model that her research colleagues had been studying. "When one begins with the study of women and derives developmental constructs from their lives, the outline of a moral conception different from that described by Freud, Piaget or Kohlberg emerges and informs a different description of development. In this conception, the moral problem arises from conflicting responsibilities rather than from competing rights and requires from its resolution a mode of thinking that is contextual and narrative rather than formal and abstract. This conception of morality as concerned with the activity of care centers moral development around the understanding of responsibility and relationships, just as the concept of morality as fairness ties moral development to the understanding of rights and rules" (Gilligan, 1982, p. 19).

Kohlberg's six-stage theory (1958, 1981), which describes moral judgment from childhood to adulthood, is based empirically on a longitudinal study of eighty-four boys followed over the course of twenty years. Women were excluded as subjects from Kohlberg's original study. Later his moral dilemmas were administered to women and sex differences were found. Kohlberg concluded from these findings that women were deficient in moral reasoning. According to Kohlberg, women appeared consistently to score at the third stage of his stage sequence. This stage is equated with helping and pleasing others. Typically, men at the same age score one stage "higher." In Kohlberg's discussion of his findings, he suggests that once women enter the traditional work arenas occupied by men, they progress like men toward higher stages where "relationships are subordinate to rules (stage four) and rules to universal principles of justice (stages five and six)" (Gilligan, 1982, p. 18).

Gilligan takes issue with this perspective on female development by arguing that there is another, equally valid approach to moral reasoning. From this alternative perspective, moral judgment based on the principle of care stresses the necessity to be responsible in relationships, to be sensitive to others' needs, and to avoid causing pain. In contrast, the traditional model of moral development described in Kohlberg's six-stage theory is based on the principle of justice, stresses separation and detachment, and considers the individual rather than the relationship as primary. Gilligan's conception of "higher stages" is not congruent with Kohlberg's sequential model.

Gilligan (1977) developed a model focusing on care. Her levels of moral development parallel Kohlberg's levels. Gilligan's model consists of three levels and is based on the interpersonal relationships in women's moral reasoning. Within level 1, the woman views moral issues from an egocentric or pragmatic point of view. As the woman begins to make a distinction between a focus on self-interests and a focus on what she should do, she begins the transition to level 2. During level 2, a woman's self-worth is based on her ability to care for others. The ability to take care of one's self is seen as dangerous in that it can hurt others and may lead to rejection from others. The transition from level 2 to level 3 is marked by a questioning of whether she should consider her own needs in addition to caring for others, as part of her commitment to care. At level 3, a woman understands and integrates a care for the self with her ability to care for others. Moral judgment takes into consideration the real physical and psychological effects of possible outcomes rather than abstract ethical principles, which from the male perspective is considered the higher order.

Gilligan stresses that both the justice and the care perspectives exist as equal but distinct orientations to dealing with moral decisions, and that they are each important in understanding human development. In her most recent work, *Mapping the Moral Domain* (Gilligan, 1989), she discusses research that clarifies and modifies her original findings and builds an argument to substantiate the need for both perspectives. She contends that the justice and care perspectives are two "ideals of human relationships" that serve as "coordinates" for viewing moral reasoning and moral emotion, and that the two more realistically account for the observed similarities and differences in male and female behavior (Gilligan, 1989, p. iv).

Gilligan holds that these two perspectives coexist in individuals, although there is a "pattern of predominance," with individuals favoring the use of one perspective over the other. This predominance, although not gender specific, is gender related and tied to differences in moral orientation that in turn relate to "ways of imagining self in relationships" (Gilligan, 1989, p. 8).

The exclusion of women in psychological research has served to silence the significance of relationships in the development of self, since men are more likely to favor the justice orientation than the care perspective. According to Gilligan this potential exclusion of relationships as a care frame of reference in the development of identity not only has caused women to feel alienated and unvalued but also has distorted the process of growth and development, rendering both men and women vulnerable to incomplete standards of behavior (Gilligan, 1989, pp. xxvii–xxxvii).

A morality of care appears to be a lifelong concern of individuals of both sexes, according to Gilligan. Her assertion is contrary to the characterization of care as a transitory stage in the Kohlberg model. Gilligan states that a definition of self in relation to others appears to occur for both sexes across all ages (Lyons, 1983). A series of studies support her contention that both men and women raise both justice and care concerns in describing moral conflict, although they tend to focus on either justice or care concerns (Gilligan and Attanucci, 1989; Lyons, 1983; Langdale, 1980). Johnston (1989) found sex differences in moral orientation, with boys more often choosing justice and girls more often choosing care strategies. Although boys and men tend to remain consistent in their preference for a rights orientation as they mature, women show an increasing tendency to choose both orientations as they mature. From this finding, Johnston (1989, p. 61) suggests that "girls may learn the dominant voice of morality, that of justice, and be able to represent this culturally valued dominant voice, but in addition, may represent a less well articulated voice of morality and shift voices with greater flexibility than boys. This flexibility may be a strength which is more evident in girls' development than in boys', and it raises the question of whether this is characteristic of girls in particular or of subordinate groups in general."

In summary, Gilligan (1989) stresses that psychologists have placed an overriding value on separation, individuation, and autonomy. Placing self-sufficiency at the pinnacle of maturity creates a view of adult development that is at odds with the human experience and divorced from our historical understanding of cultural development. According to Gilligan this limited perspective cannot accommodate the kinds of long-term commitments to and involvements with other people that actually underpin and remain central to child-rearing and education in a global society. She concludes that we need new concepts and new categories of interpretation for human development and that the accumulation of data utilizing old concepts and frames of reference perpetuates and exacerbates existing problems. She views the inclusion of the voice of care with the voice of justice as necessary to understanding the full dimensions of the concept of "self" and as central to addressing the moral issues of our times.

The Importance of Gilligan's Work to Student Development

The work of Gilligan and her associates has tremendous implications for the future of student development theory and practice. She was the first human development theorist to seriously question the universally held assumption of a singular developmental model. Although she was not the first to suggest that there are sex differences in human development, she was the first to challenge the assumption that departures from the male model reflect deficiencies or deviations.

Not only does her work challenge the theoretical assumptions of the single-sex linear model of development, it also challenges the validity of a research methodology based on detachment and objectivity as the primary variables of data collection and theory formation. The exclusion of women in the development of theory has produced a political and cultural bias that limits and distorts our understanding of the human experience. Gilligan questions the narrow, controlled, and removed methodology used in gathering data and shows how it contributes to a limited, myopic view that does not explain the full range of human behavior. She concludes that other methodologies such as those used in anthropological and historical research need to be incorporated more fully into the developmental study of human behavior and experience. Her challenges provide student development educators with an opportunity to reflect on their over-reliance on limited psychological theory and methodology in the study of student development. She urges such educators to expand their research methodologies to include qualitative designs and "more naturalistic modes of inquiry" (Delworth, Greiner, and Griffin-Pierson, 1988).

Gilligan's most significant contribution to student development theory and practice is the introduction of a new model for understanding the process of moral reasoning. Her model, which incorporates an alternative perspective of care into Kohlberg's model of justice, provides a framework for many diverse conceptions of the human experience and discounts the notion of a singular, true, and superior perspective for studying such realms of human experience as cognition, moral development, and identity formation.

Gilligan's model also raises questions about the current "mainstream" designs of campus environments and services, challenging campuses to attend to issues of inclusion-exclusion and the diversity of needs and learning styles exhibited in an expanding, heterogeneous student population. Finally, her model calls for the establishment of a new educational agenda that promotes the educational and developmental needs of a diverse population of women. (For more discussion of such a proposal, see Pearson, Shavlick, and Touchton, 1989).

Gilligan's work reinforces the importance of relationships in educational settings, pointing out the fluid nature of learning and development. It highlights the importance of connection and commitment to the learning process. Her theory provides a means of integrating and balancing the competing perspectives of interpersonal relationships and social autonomy into the scheme of human development.

A number of researchers have begun to apply Gilligan's theory to student development. Delworth (1984) discusses Gilligan's model of care and its implications for students, research, and student affairs professionals. Hotelling and Forrest (1985) outline the importance of understanding the female and the male voices in the counseling role. Stonewater (1987) integrates Gilligan's model into the process of counseling women. Forrest, Hotelling, and Kuk (1984) apply Gilligan's model of care to the use of the campus ecology model in assessing campus environment, while McCann, Sieber, and Scissors (1985) apply the care model to the issues of campus judicial systems. Gilligan's hypothesis that relationships are a key factor in the decision-making process of women is used by Mahoney and Anderson (1988) to determine how relationships affect women's decisions to enroll in college. Greeley and Tinsley (1988) compare the theories of Erikson, Chickering, and Gilligan as they characterize issues of autonomy and intimacy development in college students.

Expanding Theory and Research on Gender Awareness and Identity

Closely allied to Gilligan's work in the area of gender awareness is the resurgence of exploration in the area of epistemological development, originally conceptualized by Piaget (1928). Labeled "intellectual development" by Perry (1970), "reflective judgment" by King and Kitchener (1985), and "ways of knowing" by Belenky, Clinchy, Goldberger, and Tarule (1986), these theories and models attempt to explain how individuals perceive the world and go about "making meaning" on issues of knowledge and values.

Perry's (1970) theory, expanding on the work of Piaget, proposes nine stages of intellectual development. Like Kohlberg's work, Perry's original studies focused primarily on men, with interviews conducted over the span of their four years in college. King and Kitchener (1985), in contrast, conducted their research with a group of men and women over a period of ten years. Their seven-stage model of reflective judgment diverges significantly from Perry's model after stage 3. (For discussion of the model, see Mines and Kitchener, 1986; Rodgers, 1989). Baxter-Magolda (1988, p. 531) speculates, "It is perhaps the inclusion of gender in the model's construction that accounts for the differences between this model and Perry's scheme."

Belenky, Clinchy, Goldberger, and Tarule (1986) examined women's ways of viewing the world and making judgments about truth and knowledge. Citing the inadequacy of Perry's (1970) research on the experiences of women, they focused exclusively on women in order to examine "what else women might have to say about development of their minds and on alternative routes that are sketchy or missing in Perry's version" (1986, p. 9). Using Perry's scheme as their guide, they adopted an intense schedule of interviews and case studies to analyze the experiences of 135 women. From this qualitative approach they formulated a model containing five perspectives, which, according to the authors, are not sufficiently defined to represent cognitive stages of development. However, the perspectives do appear to increase in complexity and are similar to Perry's first five stages. Their findings evidence the existence of parallel structural development, with some qualitative differences in the way women, in contrast to men, deal with the transition from uncertainty to certainty in epistemological development.

Research on gender difference using the reflective judgment model has been divided, leaving answers to the question of sex differences unclear. However, some data suggest that men score slightly higher than women on measures of reflective judgment and that this difference increases with age and education (King and Kitchener, 1985). Baxter-Magolda (1988) found evidence to support varying dimensions of all three models (Perry, 1970; King and Kitchener, 1985; Belenky, Clinchy, Goldberger, and Tarule, 1986), and although her results are limited, they support the "hypothesis that qualitative gender differences exist within parallel cognitive structures" (Baxter-Magolda, 1988, p. 536). Additional longitudinal studies are needed to clearly resolve these issues.

How women go about forming their individual identities is another area of gender awareness research that has emerged in connection with the work of Gilligan. Erikson (1950, 1956, 1968) postulated that the lifecycle consists of eight hierarchical stages dealing progressively with the resolution of identity development. Like many other researchers, Erikson concentrated almost exclusively on men, except for his suggestion that much of a woman's identity resides in her choice of the men by whom she wants to be pursued (1968). Josselson (1987) takes issue with Erikson and speculates that women, based on their need for relationships, proceed in their identity development differently than men. Utilizing the research model developed by Marcia (1966), which refined Erikson's theory in order to make it amenable to criteria of empirical validation, she conducted a longitudinal study of thirty-four women over a twelve-year period. Her findings suggest that the aspects of experience important to identity formation in women have been overlooked by psychological research and theory, which stress the growth of independence and autonomy. Josselson (1987, p. 191) found that women construct identity around issues of "communion, connection, relational embeddedness, spirituality, and affiliation," resulting in an identity that is uniquely female in form.

Although it is still too early to draw conclusions about the extent of gender differences in these developmental processes, the findings to date do support Gilligan's contention that relationships and a concern for others are key developmental components that have been overlooked in previous research. Developmental differences in how we view ourselves in relation to others may be gender related. The process of development and the environmental context are related to gender and are critical to the emergence of healthy, well-balanced, responsible adults, whether male or female.

Implications for Future Study and Practice

Delworth, Greiner, and Griffin-Pierson (1988) discuss the importance of the new scholarship on women and its implications for student development services, research, and education. They propose six tenets that provide a woman's voice in our understanding of relevant theory, research, and practice in student affairs (Delworth, Greiner, and Griffin-Pierson, 1988, pp. 485, 511): (1) Women and men are viewed as whole persons, composed of biological, ecological, psychological, social, and political aspects. (2) The study of each group is valued for its own sake and need not be compared to another group. (3) The use of the dialectic and a feminist process of egalitarianism are essential to the new perspective (Hanson, 1988, pp. 501–503). (4) The naturalistic mode of inquiry, rather than the scientific and positivist mode, provides the framework. (5) Values are consistently explored in research and practice. (6) Phenomena are embedded in context (Greiner, 1988, p. 485).

We now stand at the threshold of a new understanding of student development. The six tenets above will serve as valuable tools in directing the methods and modes of our scholarship. They are key elements in shaping a new research agenda that will steer the student affairs profession beyond outdated and limited notions of human development theory and student development practice into a new paradigm of understanding. Such a new understanding will provide a clearer developmental framework for addressing the needs of women, and it will guide how we view our work, our relationships, and our campuses.

This new understanding will engage us in the process of discovering new ways to integrate the many facets of our lives, with balance between our competing needs for autonomy and relationships. It will deflect our attention and energy away from reliance on a singular process of education and development and toward establishment of multiple perspectives on the variety and broad scope of learning styles and ways of knowing. It will cause us to relinquish old notions of morality that focus on a singular perspective of justice and to adopt new notions that incorporate the multiple dimensions of care and justice, thereby reshaping the way we interact as persons and as nations.

The emergence of gender as a variable of difference has raised the question, What else is missing? With the stimulus provided by Gilligan and her feminist colleagues, the reliance on a singular, linear theory of development to explain all human experience is waning. A redesign of theory is underway that will include the multiple dimensions of gender, race, culture, and sexual orientation, reflecting a more realistic expression of the human experience and a more solid and enduring framework to use in shaping student development practice.

References

Baker-Miller, J. *Toward a New Psychology of Women.* Boston: Beacon, 1976.

Baker-Miller, J. *Toward a New Psychology of Women.* (2nd ed.) Boston: Beacon, 1986.

Baxter-Magolda, M. B. "Measuring Gender Differences in Intellectual Development: A Comparison of Assessment Methods." *Journal of College Student Development,* 1988, *29,* 528–537.

Belenky, M. F., Clinchy, B. M., Goldberger, N. R., and Tarule, J. M. *Women's Ways of Knowing: The Development of Self, Voice, and Mind.* New York: Basic Books, 1986.

Chodorow, N. *The Reproduction of Mothering: Psychoanalysis and the Sociology of Gender.* Berkeley: University of California Press, 1978.

Delworth, U. "The Ethics of Care: Implications of Gilligan for the Student Services Profession." *Journal of College Student Personnel,* 1984, *25,* 489–492.

Delworth, U., Greiner, M., and Griffin-Pierson, S. (eds.). *Journal of College Student Development,* 1988, *29,* 484–511, including "Toward a More Abundant Construction," p. 511.

Erikson, E. H. *Childhood and Society.* New York: Norton, 1950.

Erikson, E. H. "The Problem of Ego Identity." *Journal of the American Psychoanalytic Association,* 1956, *4,* 56–121.

Erikson, E. H. *Identity: Youth and Crisis.* New York: Norton, 1968.

Forrest, L., Hotelling, K., and Kuk, L. "The Elimination of Sexism in the University Environment." Paper presented at the second annual Campus Ecology symposium, Pengree Park, Colorado, June 25–29, 1984.

Freud, S. *Three Essays on the Theory of Sexuality.* London: Imazo, 1905.

Gilligan, C. "In a Different Voice: Women's Conceptions of the Self and of Morality." *Harvard Educational Review,* 1977, *47,* 481–517.

Gilligan, C. *In a Different Voice.* Cambridge, Mass.: Harvard University Press, 1982.

Gilligan, C. (ed.). *Mapping the Moral Domain.* Cambridge, Mass.: Harvard University Press, 1989.

Gilligan, C., and Attanucci, J. "Two Moral Orientations." In C. Gilligan (ed.), *Mapping the Moral Domain.* Cambridge, Mass.: Harvard University Press, 1989.

Greely, A. T., and Tinsley, H.E.A. "Autonomy and Intimacy Development in College Students: Sex Differences and Predictions." *Journal of College Student Development,* 1988, *29,* 512–520.

Greiner, M. "The New Scholarship on Women: An Innovative Perspective for Student Affairs." *Journal of College Student Development,* 1988, *29,* 485–491.

Hall, R. M., and Sandler, B. *The Classroom Climate: A Chilly One for Women?* Washington, D.C.: Project on the Status and Education of Women, Association of American Colleges, 1982.

Hanson, G. R. "These Truths Are Self-Evident, But. . . ." *Journal of College Student Development,* 1988, *29,* 501–503.

Hotelling, K., and Forrest, L. "Gilligan's Theory of Sex Role Development: A Perspective for Counseling." *Journal of Counseling and Development,* 1985, *64* (3), 183–186.

Johnston, K. "Adolescents' Solutions to Dilemmas in Fables: Two Moral Orientations—Two Problem-Solving Strategies." In C. Gilligan (ed.), *Mapping the Moral Domain.* Cambridge, Mass.: Harvard University Press, 1989.

Josselson, R. *Finding Herself: Pathways to Identity Development in Women.* San Francisco: Jossey-Bass, 1987.

King, P. M., and Kitchener, K. S. "Reflective Judgment Theory and Research: Insights into the Process of Knowing in the College Years." Paper presented at the annual meeting of the American College Personnel Association, Boston, March 24–27, 1985.

Kohlberg, L. "The Development of Modes of Thinking and Choices in Years 10 to 16." Unpublished doctoral dissertation, University of Chicago, 1958.

Kohlberg, L. "Stage and Sequence: The Cognitive-Developmental Approach to Socialization." In D. A. Goslin (ed.), *Handbook of Socialization Theory and Research.* Skokie, Ill.: Rand McNally, 1969.

Kohlberg, L. *The Philosophy of Moral Development.* San Francisco: Harper & Row, 1981.

Langdale, S. "Moral Orientations and Moral Development: The Analysis of Care and Justice Reasoning Across Different Dilemmas in Females and Males from Childhood Through Adulthood." Unpublished doctoral dissertation, Graduate School of Education, Harvard University, 1980.

Lyons, N. P. "Two Perspectives: On Self, Relationships, and Morality." *Harvard Educational Review,* 1983, *53,* 125–145.

McCann, J., Sieber, C., and Scissor, C. "Using Gilligan's Theory to Redesign University Judicial Systems." Paper presented at the third annual Campus Ecology Symposium, Pingree Park, Colorado, June 1985.

Mahoney, C., and Anderson, W. "The Effects of Life Events and Relationships on Adult Women's Decisions to Enroll in College." *Journal of Counseling and Development,* 1988, *6,* 271–274.

Marcia, J. E. "Development and Validation of Ego Identity Status." *Journal of Personality and Social Psychology,* 1966, *3,* 551–558.

Mines, R. A., and Kitchener, K. S. *Adult Cognitive Development: Methods and Models.* New York: Praeger, 1986.

Pearson, C. S., Shavlick, D. I., and Touchton, J. G. *Educating the Majority: Women Challenge Tradition in Higher Education.* New York: American Council on Education and Macmillan, 1989.

Perry, W. G. *Forms of Intellectual and Ethical Development in the College Years.* New York: Holt, Rinehart & Winston, 1968.

Piaget, J. *The Child's Conception of the World.* London: Routledge & Kegan Paul.

Piaget, J. *The Origins of Intelligence in Children.* New York: International Universities Press, 1952.

Rich, A. "Toward a Women-Centered University." In F. Howe (ed.), *Women and the Power to Change.* New York: McGraw-Hill, 1975.

Rodgers, R. F. "Student Development." In U. Delworth and G. R. Hanson (eds.), *Student Services: A Handbook for the Profession.* (2nd ed.) San Francisco: Jossey-Bass, 1989.

Schaef, A. W. *Women's Reality.* Minneapolis, Minn.: Winston Press, 1981.

Stonewater, B. B. "Career Traits, Decision Style and Gilligan: Implications for Counseling Women." *Journal of the National Association for Women Deans, Administrators and Counselors,* 1987, *50* (3), 17–26.

Linda Kuk is currently vice-president for student affairs at the State University of New York College, Cortland. In addition to her responsibilities as an administrator, she teaches adolescent development and serves as an organization consultant.

The presence of adult learners on college campuses highlights the need to understand concepts of life span development, the process of revisiting psychosocial themes, and the nature of transitions.

Perspectives on Age Differences

LuAnn Krager, Robert Wrenn, Joan Hirt

This chapter addresses the contributions that increasing numbers of persons have made to our awareness of college student and life span development simply by entering higher education after the age of twenty-four. Once thought an anomaly, older students are growing in number, and with the rise in presence their needs and characteristics have increasingly received attention. Resultant research has not only enhanced the knowledge base about the "older than expected" college participant but also signaled to those interested in life span development that more adults are making choices that defy their age- and stage-predicted activities.

We present here an overview of the older adult population, including definition, demographics, and illustrative characteristics. With this base, the discussion turns to the impact older students have had on developmental theory and its application to college students of all ages.

Definition

Anyone entering college who is not a recent high school graduate is still considered, in some sense, different from the typical student. The farther one departs from the age, experience, and societal expectations of going directly from high school to college, the more difficult it can be to feel supported in the desire to receive a college education. Little more than a decade ago, a variety of terms were used to describe those students who were older than the expected age of eighteen to twenty-four years. The labels "returning," "reentry," and "nontraditional" were just a few of the adjectives applied to this population. In fact, Kurland (1978) identified more than thirty terms in use at that time in reference to older students.

In recent years, more focused research has resulted in a narrower definition of the older college student. Most experts now tend to use the common labels of "nontraditional student" or "adult learner." The reference typically describes students twenty-five years of age or older, enrolled in degree or certification programs offered by colleges and universities, or completing coursework leading to admission to such programs (Aslanian and Pollack, 1983; Kelly, 1986; Rogers, Gilleland, and Dixon, 1987; Silling, 1984).

The term adult learner has increased in usage even though student development professionals also view traditionally aged students as having adult status and interact with them in a manner that expects and promotes increasing maturity and self-responsibility. Recent demographics underscore the reality that the term nontraditional, once appropriately heralding the uniqueness of this population, no longer applies to older students by virtue of both their sizable numbers on college campuses and the choices they are making with respect to higher education. For this discussion, then, the term adult learner is used to refer to this important population.

Demographics and Trends

Changes in the demographics of students enrolled in colleges and universities have been well documented in the literature and are remarkably consistent when data are viewed collectively. Lace (1986) reported that 43 percent of students enrolled in postsecondary institutions in 1985 were twenty-five years of age or older, and that by 1993 the adult learner will comprise 49 percent of enrollment. Silling (1984) presented a 1981 report stating that 33 percent of all students enrolled in credit coursework were age twenty-five or older, and projecting that this proportion of adult learners would increase to nearly 50 percent by 1990. Although the projected proportion of adult learners has not reached the 50 percent estimate, it is safe to say that roughly 42 percent of the student population is adult learners.

The United States Department of Education recently conducted its first comprehensive survey of enrollment by age level (Evangelauf, 1989). Of the 12,786,307 students attending higher education institutions in the fall of 1987, 21.2 percent of all full-time students and 66.8 percent of all part-time students were over age twenty-four. Overall, adult learners comprised 40.9 percent of all college students.

Clearly, there has been a significant shift in the age demographics of college and university students in the past decade. Given the patterns of differential birth rates and the general aging of the American population (Hodgkinson, 1983), it is likely that the percentage of adult learners on campuses will continue to rise and, ultimately, become the majority of those enrolled in such settings.

Characteristics of the Adult Learner

Most older students are not distracted from the pursuit of higher education by having to learn how to function on their own for the first time. Having been responsible to employer or family demands, the older student has an edge on the recent high school graduate toward succeeding in college. The passage of years can also bring doubts, loss, and varied and complex roles and responsibilities. The effects of life experience are consistently present in the literature devoted to describing the characteristics of adult college students.

Richter-Antion (1986), for example, offers five factors that distinguish adult students from their younger counterparts: greater sense of purpose, better understanding of the financial and time commitments required in higher education, diverse life experiences, lack of age cohort, and broader concept of social responsibility. Other population descriptors have included broader life experiences; stronger commitments to educational goals; better concept of time; greater self-direction, responsibility, and motivation; stronger sense of self; and greater experience with informal learning such as that garnered from newspapers, television, and social activities (Martin, 1988; Silling, 1984; Swift, Colvin, and Mills, 1987).

Stronger sense of purpose is not without its challenges. The choice of adult learners to attend college frequently results in some amount of sacrifice, including costs to family, work, leisure time, and finances. Moreover, upon entering the college environment, adult learners often have confusion about relating to authority, question their abilities in the college setting, and experience a significant amount of flux in their lives (Aslanian and Pollack, 1983).

Although studies agree that motivations are complex and individualized, Sewell's (1986) survey of adult students showed 65 percent of the respondents "wanted to develop a new career," 62 percent enrolled "simply to learn," and 51 percent wanted "to have the satisfaction of having a degree." Research also indicates a higher proportion of female adult students than is normally assumed are motivated by career goals (Hooper and Traupmann, 1984; St. Pierre, 1989).

Much of the literature that relates specifically to age awareness of the older college student has to do with women. Even with this gender specificity, Adelstein, Sedlacek, and Martinez (1983) caution that adult female learners should not be homogeneously characterized, suggesting that the various subpopulations, for example, older family women and career-oriented women, must be studied and described individually. Their point is well taken and should be considered with male and ethnic minority subpopulations as well.

It appears the most consistent common motivator of college attendance for any group of adult learners is a life change event (Knox, 1980), or state of transition (Schlossberg, 1984, 1987; Schlossberg, Lynch, and Chickering, 1989). Whether the transition is initiated by a structured event, such as divorce, last child entering school, or job layoff, or by a nonevent, such as the boredom and stagnation that prompts persons to make a drastic change to get more from life, the act of entering college also means entering a time of significant personal change.

Developmental Theory

Age awareness has been an impetus for close scrutiny of existing developmental theory in general and the application of psychosocial theory in particular. Psychosocial theory addresses the "what" of people's thoughts rather than the "how" of cognitive development. Erikson (1959, 1968) began discussion of the life span with his seminal charting of the human life-cycle, composed of eight ego development stages.

Chapter One of this volume offers a detailed historical and theoretical overview of major contributions to developmental study, including those of Erikson. For present purposes, it is sufficient to note that each life-cycle stage in Erikson's theory is focused on a basic issue, conceptualized as a pair of polar attitudes toward life. Consistent with descriptions of development in cognitive theories, the differentiation and integration of inconsistency work to resolve conflict and promote progress to the next stage.

Resolution of the issue emerges as a quality of ego functioning. The eight stages and the conflict quality in need of resolution are the following: trust versus mistrust (hope), autonomy versus doubt (will), initiative versus guilt (purpose), industry versus inferiority (competence), identity versus role confusion (fidelity), intimacy versus isolation (love), generativity versus stagnation (care), and integrity versus despair or disgust (wisdom). The eight stages are respectively related to the ages of infancy; early, middle, and late childhood; adolescence; young adulthood; and maturity.

Influenced by Erikson, Chickering (1969) expanded the stage of adolescent identity to include sources of influence that must be resolved in order to formulate identity and the self's role in the world. He proposes seven vectors of growth during adolescence: developing competence, managing emotions, developing autonomy, establishing identity, freeing interpersonal relationships, clarifying purpose, and developing integrity.

Other theorists, following Erikson's lead, focus specifically on the adult years. They have expanded and embellished the broad growth themes to acknowledge and describe the common tasks or activities that are confronted in adulthood, including family and work roles. Prominent writers about adult learners include Gould (1977, 1978), Knowles (1979), Knox (1977), and Levinson (1978).

Initially, then, interest in the adult years brought a flurry of discussion, with growing specificity, about predictable age-related activities. Social changes, however, including birth and divorce rates, single parenting, mobility, gender equity, technological advances phasing careers in and out, and financial assistance programs, have motivated older students to expand their lives through traditional degree programs. With growing numbers of older students appearing on college campuses, student affairs professionals have sought to discern what is still applicable in current developmental theory for the adult learner.

New Views of Theory Use

Changes in the student population and data on special subpopulations have led to new ways of viewing theory. This section reexamines current theoretical notions and considers the emergence of new models for developmental application.

The Concept of Recycling and Revisiting Psychosocial Themes. Erikson, in his earlier work, had stated that while all eight ego qualities were present in any given stage, the appropriate age-related stage would be in ascendancy. In later elaboration, he posed the spiraling nature of life-cycle issues (Erikson, 1981). This concept that life-cycle issues are not limited to linear development has produced a paradigm shift in our theory. Erikson's 1981 assertion, for example, suggests that although college students of traditional age are likely preoccupied with industry, identity, and intimacy, a "recycling" due to the impact of life events can cause a revisiting of preceding stages.

Expanding on the suggestion of recycling throughout the life-cycle, any significant life event can promote a return to earlier themes. For example, the eighteen-year-old college student leaves family and friends for the first time and must learn to trust self and others (trust), initiate control (autonomy), apply efforts (initiative), and achieve (competence) in a new environment. These themes may also be evident in the student affairs practitioner who, after completing a graduate program, moves into a new region, climate, setting, and career position. The same themes could also confront the adult student reentering the structure of formal education after experiencing a job layoff, death of a spouse, or divorce.

It is not surprising that two characteristics in particular emerge in adult learners when they enter college. These characteristics are mistrust of abilities in the college setting and confusion over relations with authority. The concept of recycling suggests the reworking of trust, autonomy, initiative, and competence as adult learners build and qualify their identities as college students in conjunction with other life roles.

It must be noted that Erikson's work has received pertinent criticism in recent years on its applicability to women (Evans, 1985). Chapter Two of this volume offers relevant discussion of female socialization and its impact on the development of identity and intimacy, material that must be included in the full consideration of human development. Whether or not gender roles condition differences in the unfolding of identity and intimacy, the concept of recycling warrants emphasis in any reexamination of life span themes in relation to individuals facing significant change.

Recycling is not just a return to a previous stage but a revisiting of themes in qualitatively and quantitatively different ways. Progress through the revisiting is dependent on the individual and the context. Consider a woman who has never worked outside the home facing a husband who initiates divorce after thirty-five years of marriage. She will most likely have a more demanding journey through trust and autonomous self-reliance in ending her relationship than will the woman of a dual-career couple or the twenty-year-old college student with an active social life.

Rather than incorporating age-related themes only into a model of student development, practitioners would be wise to rethink the impact of the new environment on all students. The process of Erikson's growth themes, trust through identity, could be shaped into questions that promote examination of student issues and evaluation of professional programs and responses. A student sorting through issues of trust, for instance, is likely to view the environment through the filter of "Who or what can I trust? Can I trust me?" Autonomy issues might be stated as "Over what or whom do I have control? What/who has control over me? Do I have the strength, courage, 'the will' to act, govern, direct even me?"

The stage of initiative blends the trust in, and hope for, a predictable consequence with the autonomy of independent action. "Is it trustworthy enough to predict? To put effort toward? Am I? Are others?" Students want to hope that actions and efforts can produce change. The stage of industry can be described as bringing questions of quality and quantity to the efforts established in initiative. "Do I have the ability and the stamina to achieve my goal? To succeed?" Lastly, identity issues prompt "Who am I in this new setting? Who should I associate with? What should I be like? Who do I want to be? Am I who I say I am?"

Chickering also has elaborated on his theory's application. In recent work, he provided a summary of characteristics distinguishing the adult learner from students aged eighteen to twenty-four (Lynch and Chickering, 1984; Thomas and Chickering, 1984; Schlossberg, Lynch, and Chickering, 1989). In his description, adult learners have a wider range of individual differences, which are more sharply determined, than the differences among younger students. They face multiple demands and responsibilities, including family and work, that affect time constraints, energy, emotions, and roles. They have more concern for practical application and less patience for pure theory and abstractions. Chickering adds that older students have a greater self-responsibility and a greater need to cope with transitions and existential issues related to each of his seven vectors.

Similar to the concept of recycling when life events prompt themes to reemerge, Chickering's description acknowledges that older students may be experiencing the same issues faced by their younger colleagues. Adaption to the newness and uniqueness of the college setting is a potent force for change, one sufficiently strong to be an impetus for the revisiting of developmental issues in new ways. The sorting and resolving of those issues, of course, are tempered and affected by the varied individual experiences, multiple demands, practicality, and responsibility that appear to be characteristic of the adult student's life.

Research on the adult learner as well as the expanding data base on all student populations have prompted the construction of new student development models. The compilation and integration of research knowledge, developmental literature, and population characteristics allow a more informed look at particular students and the general student population. The following models are presented with all students in mind, although illustrations are designed especially for adult learners.

A Model Addressing Transition. The adult learner has been characterized as one whose life is often in flux. Schlossberg offers student development professionals a model for understanding the impact of change on, and for analyzing the needs and resources of, the individual in transition (Schlossberg, 1984, 1987; Schlossberg, Lynch, and Chickering, 1989).

According to Schlossberg, there is no single, predictable, universal adult experience. Rather, there are many, and they frequently involve transitions. It is thus more important to know that a person is a newlywed or recently divorced than it is to know their chronological age. In her analysis, how a transition influences an individual's growth, including the alteration of roles, relationships, routines, and assumptions, depends on the nature and strength of impact of the transition.

There are anticipated transitions such as marrying or entering college, unanticipated transitions such as an injury or a job promotion, and nonevent transitions, which are expected events that do not occur such as the failure to secure a coveted job. Schlossberg suggests that by examining four contextual categories of transition, we can better understand how individuals cope with life changes and what helping role practitioners might assume. The four categories are *situation, self, supports,* and *strategies.*

The situation includes where a person is in a transition, "moving in, moving through, or moving on," and whether the person views the transition as positive or negative, "on" or "off" time, and voluntary or imposed. Assessment should also question whether this is a personal transition, or a reaction to someone else's. Analysis of the self involves the individual's strengths for coping, including previous experience in a similar transition, ability to see options, optimism, and tolerance for ambiguity. Transition supports are external variables such as financial assets and emotional assistance from others. Finally, strategies include the number and type of avenues used constructively to modify the situation. This category emphasizes that there is usually no single answer to the question of how to cope. Rather, there are multiple strategies that can be utilized creatively to change the situation, or the meaning of it.

Schlossberg offers the student development professional a model that stresses the need for individualized assessment when a transition occurs. Although the model can be applied to all students, regardless of age, Schlossberg's particular conception of transition is designed to meet the additional complexity of roles and responsibilities present in the adult learner population.

The Mission Paradigm. Another recent model for promoting and assessing student development was initially applied in the field of residence life education (Jakobsen and Krager, 1986, 1988) and later modified for use across student affairs divisions (Andreas and Krager, 1989). The model is a four-category framework based on a synthesis of Perry, Gilligan, Piaget, Erikson, Chickering, Kohlberg, and other developmental theorists. Its authors refer to it as the Mission Paradigm. The Mission is based on development and learning theory, with an interjection of definitions solicited from students, faculty, and administrators about the "educated person."

Thus, the framework categories were created as a theory-driven mission statement formulated for practical application. The categories include (1) developing a sense of belonging (affiliation and community), (2) acquiring knowledge and skills (cognitive development and applied problem solving), (3) choosing informed attitudes (emotional and ethical development), and (4) assuming self-responsibility (fostering behavioral commitment).

Each category has a hierarchy of fourteen to eighteen desired student outcomes that provides a general guide to and assessment of growth processes and direction. Each student outcome is a behavioral description of a level of achieved growth. The difference between any two descriptors suggests the type of intervention needed to challenge the student to move onward to another developmental level.

In creating the Mission Paradigm, Jakobsen and Krager emphasized the themes of development that are consistent across theories rather than specific to one age or stage theory. They have incorporated cognitive and psychosocial development as well as themes involving ethical decision making and environmental impact. The Mission provides an organized compilation that can guide intervention as well as direct the construction of a cocurriculum. The categories and outcomes are used in conjunction with data on special populations (for example, ethnic minority, international, age, gender) and on individuals.

As with Schlossberg's contribution on transitions, the Mission framework is applicable to all students. As illustration, the general categories can easily prompt questions for the practitioner regarding adult learners. For example, are efforts made to promote a sense of belonging on campus for the adult learner? Schlossberg and Warren (1985) consistently found that when adult learners felt they mattered to an adviser, or to an institution, this sense of belonging kept them engaged in learning. Similarly, are the learning characteristics and interests of adults, such as increased practicality, application of personal experience, information that can be used on their own time, and extended hours for resources, utilized to assist them in acquiring skills and knowledge? Are the adults assisted in choosing informed attitudes as they encounter new life roles and information? Knox (1980) describes older learners as having a strong interest in culture and personal introspection. Finally, as programs are offered to younger college students in assuming self-responsibility, are adult learners also assisted with balancing responsibilities when commitments are strong yet not easily aligned?

Summary

Recent demographics indicate approximately 21 percent of all full-time students and 67 percent of all part-time students at higher education institutions are over the age of twenty-four. With this increase in adult learners, student affairs professionals have started to reexamine existing theory on college student and adult development. There is well-deserved emphasis on the adult learner with new models that describe this population and suggest professional responses.

In the midst of social change and an increasingly diverse college population, it appears that student affairs practitioners must develop an expanded approach to applied theory and research. First, they must synthesize from theoretical contributions an understanding of what is similar for all students during their pursuit of learning in a relatively unfamiliar environment. Second, they must utilize data on different subpopulations in an effort to adapt to and underscore special needs, when and where appropriate. Third, they must continue to organize concepts and data into meaningful guides for themselves as well as into learning objectives for students. The models reviewed here are illustrations of needed integration. Assuredly, new models will follow. The challenge is to utilize them in ways that in principle and in practice serve the needs of all students in our institutions of higher education.

References

Adelstein, D., Sedlacek, W. E., and Martinez, A. "Dimensions Underlying the Characteristics and Needs of Returning Women Students." *NAWDAC* (National Association of Woman Deans, Administrators, and Counselors) *Journal,* 1983, 47, 32–37.

Andreas, R., and Krager, L. "Dissemination of a Student Development Model Within a Student Life Unit." Paper presented at the Arizona AzCPA-NASPA Joint Conference, Tucson, April 20–21, 1989.

Aslanian, C. B., and Pollack, R. W. *Improving Financial Aid Services for Adults: A Program Guide.* New York: College Entrance Examination Board, 1983.

Chickering, A. W. *Education and Identity.* San Francisco: Jossey-Bass, 1969.

Erikson, E. H. *Identity and the Life Cycle: Psychological Issues.* New York: International Universities Press, 1959.

Erikson, E. H. *Identity: Youth and Crisis.* New York: Norton, 1968.

Erikson, E. H. "On Generativity and Identity: From a Conversation with Erik and Joan Erikson." *Harvard Educational Review,* 1981, *51* (2), 249–269.

Evangelauf, J. "More than Half of All 1987 College Students Were 22 or over, U.S. Reports." *Chronicle of Higher Education,* June 28, 1989, pp. A21, A24.

Evans, N. J. (ed.). *Facilitating the Development of Women.* New Directions for Student Services, no. 29. San Francisco: Jossey-Bass, 1985.

Gould, R. L. "The Phases of Adult Life: A Study in Developmental Psychology." In L. R. Allman and D. T. Jaffe (eds.), *Readings in Adult Psychology: Contemporary Perspectives.* New York: Harper & Row, 1977.

Gould, R. L. *Transformations: Growth and Change in Adult Life.* New York: Simon & Schuster, 1978.

Hodgkinson, H. L. *Guess Who's Coming to College: Your Students in 1990.* Washington, D.C.: National Association of Independent Colleges and Universities, 1983.

Hooper, J. O., and Traupmann, J. "Women Students over 50: Why Do They Do It?" *Journal of College Student Personnel,* 1984, *25,* 171–172.

Jakobsen, L., and Krager, L. *The Housing Paradigm: University of Nebraska–Lincoln Residential Education Mission Statement.* Register of Copyrights, Library of Congress, Washington, D.C., 1986.

Jakobsen, L., and Krager, L. "A Mission for Residential Education." *Journal of College Student Development,* 1988, *29* (5), 476–477.

Kelly, D. "Adult Learners: Implications for Faculty." Unpublished seminar paper, Claremont Graduate School, Claremont, Calif., 1986.

Knowles, M. *The Adult Learner: A Neglected Species.* (2nd ed.) Houston, Tex.: Gulf, 1979.

Knox, A. B. *Adult Development and Learning: A Handbook on Individual Growth and Competence in the Adult Years.* San Francisco: Jossey-Bass, 1977.

Knox, A. B. "Understanding the Adult Learner." In A. Shriberg (ed.), *Providing Student Services for the Adult Learner.* New Directions for Student Services, no. 11. San Francisco: Jossey-Bass, 1980.

Kurland, N. D. "A Rational Strategy for Lifelong Learning." *Phi Delta Kappan,* 1978, *59* (6), 385–389.

Lace, W. W. "A Nontraditional Approach." *Currents,* 1986, *12* (5), 8–11.

Levinson, D. *The Seasons of a Man's Life.* New York: Knopf, 1978.

Lynch, A. Q., and Chickering, A. W. "Comprehensive Counseling and Support Programs for Adult Learners: Challenge to Higher Education." In G. W. Walz and L. Benjamin (eds.), *New Perspectives on Counseling Adult Learners.* Ann Arbor, Mich.: ERIC/CAPS, 1984.

Martin, J. Y. "Meeting Nontraditional Students Halfway." *Journal of College Student Development,* 1988, *29,* 369–371.

Richter-Antion, D. "Qualitative Differences Between Adult and Younger Students." *NASPA Journal,* 1986, *23* (3), 58–62.

Rogers, B. H., Gilleland, K. R., and Dixon, G. "Educational Motivations of Part-Time Adults as Related to Social Demographic Variables." Paper presented at the annual meeting of the American Educational Research Association, Washington, D.C., April 20–25, 1987.

St. Pierre, S. "Understanding the Nontraditional Female Student." *NASPA Journal,* 1989, *26* (3), 227–234.

Schlossberg, N. K. *Counseling Adults in Transition.* New York: Springer, 1984.
Schlossberg, N. K. "Taking the Mystery Out of Change." *Psychology Today,* 1987, *21* (5), 74–75.
Schlossberg, N. K., Lynch, A. Q., and Chickering, A. W. *Improving Higher Education Environments for Adults: Responsive Programs and Services from Entry to Departure.* San Francisco: Jossey-Bass, 1989.
Schlossberg, N. K., and Warren, B. *Growing Up Adult: Reactions to Nontraditional Learning Experiences.* Columbia, Md.: Council for Advancement of Experiential Learning, 1985.
Sewell, T. J. "Nontraditionals in a Traditional Setting: Why Older Adults Return to College." Paper presented at the annual meeting of the American Educational Research Association, San Francisco, April 1986.
Silling, M. A. "Student Services for Adult Learners." Paper presented at the annual conference of the Williams Midwest Region of Academic Affairs Administrators, Dayton, Ohio, October 4–5, 1984.
Swift, J. S., Colvin, C., and Mills, D. "Displaced Homemakers: Adults Returning to College with Different Characteristics and Needs." *Journal of College Student Personnel,* 1987, *28,* 343–350.
Thomas, R., and Chickering, A. W. "Education and Identity Revisited." *Journal of College Student Personnel,* 1984, *25,* 392–399.

LuAnn Krager is an educational psychologist and currently dean of students at the University of Arizona, Tucson.

Robert Wrenn is a counseling psychologist and director of the Student Resource Center at the University of Arizona, Tucson.

Joan Hirt is a doctoral student in the Center for the Study for Higher Education and an assistant in the Dean of Students Office at the University of Arizona, Tucson.

Sexual identity development theory suggests that gay men and women who are struggling to define themselves sexually may be focused on substantially different developmental issues than are heterosexual men and women.

Perspectives on Sexual Orientation

Nancy Evans, Heidi Levine

There is a growing need on our college and university campuses to increase attention to gay, lesbian, and bisexual students by providing personal and institutional support and by educating heterosexual students and staff about homosexuality (DeVito, 1981). The need for support has been made more urgent by recent violence against gay, lesbian, and bisexual students, perhaps as a result of the growing conservative atmosphere and the fear of AIDS (which is associated in the minds of many with the gay population) (Bourassa and Cullen, 1988). Although the number of organizations for gay, lesbian, and bisexual students have increased, they often function without official administrative support. Indeed, a recent study reported that only forty-seven universities in the United States provided institutional support by banning discrimination based on sexual orientation (Bendet, 1986).

While no accurate report has been made of the number of gay, lesbian, and bisexual college students, the original Kinsey reports (Kinsey, Pomeroy, and Martin, 1948; Kinsey, Pomeroy, Martin, and Beghard, 1953) still provide the most extensive nationwide data concerning sexual behavior. These reports indicated that in the 1940s 10 percent of the men surveyed had engaged in predominantly homosexual behavior for at least three years. The incidence of reported homosexual behavior for women during that time was from one-half to one-third that of men. A more recent study conducted by the Kinsey Institute (Bell, Weinberg, and Hammersmith, 1981) found that the college years were a time of unstable sexual orientation. At the very least, we can conclude from these reports that gay, lesbian, and bisexual students (and those experiencing confusion about their sexual orientation) could benefit from the support of student affairs professionals who are well-informed about the issues faced by this population.

Unfortunately, little information about homosexuality or gay identity development is readily accessible to student affairs professionals. A recently published student affairs bibliography (Belson and Stamatakos, 1988) listed only thirteen articles on these topics. Most of the information available on gay identity formation is found in the sociological and psychological literature, particularly in journals devoted to the study of sexuality. To make matters even more difficult, many libraries have only limited holdings related to homosexuality.

To begin to fill this knowledge gap, this chapter addresses the developmental issues faced by college students who identify themselves as gay, lesbian, or bisexual; briefly reviews research and theory concerning homosexuality; and examines models of gay identity development, focusing particularly on the work of Vivienne Cass. Implications for the student affairs practice and future directions for research on gay identity development are proposed.

Developmental Issues Related to Gay Identity

Existing models of student and adult development, such as those of Chickering (1969), Erikson (1975), and Levinson (1978), are based on an assumption that all individuals are heterosexual. These and other theorists discuss issues, such as lifestyle development and development of intimate relationships, with this bias toward heterosexuality. Only a few writers (Kimmel, 1978; Sohier, 1985–1986) have attempted to modify existing developmental theory to include gay, lesbian, and bisexual individuals. Others (Martin, 1982; Weinberg, 1983) have noted that developmental issues such as building self-esteem, developing social skills, and maintaining a sense of identity may be particularly difficult for adolescents who are struggling at the same time to define themselves sexually.

The effects of this struggle on a young person who experiences confusion about sexual orientation can be devastating. According to a National Institute of Mental Health study (Adams, 1989), as many as 30 percent of the teenagers who eventually commit suicide identify themselves as gay or lesbian. Additionally, Scott (1988) suggests that gay students face some unique developmental issues, such as dealing with discrimination, harassment, and rejection. These issues are similar in some ways to those faced by members of racial and ethnic minorities (see Chapter Five of this volume).

The college years are particularly crucial to the identity development of gay, lesbian, and bisexual students, as well as to the development of heterosexual students' attitudes about homosexuality. Most gay, lesbian, and bisexual individuals become aware of their orientation during late adolescence or early adulthood, and they establish their first serious relationship in their early twenties (Bell and Weinberg, 1978; Sohier, 1985–1986). Accurate information about sexuality and a healthy social environment form the foundation for developing a positive identity (Martin, 1982). For heterosexual students, college may provide their first exposure to openly gay students, thereby affording the opportunity for them to break down stereotypes and become more tolerant and sensitive to diversity (Bourassa and Cullen, 1988).

Research and Theory About Homosexuality

The scientific study of homosexuality began around 1945. From its inception, it has been mostly male oriented and conducted mainly in America (Plummer, 1981). Early studies focused on determining the causes of homosexuality in order to treat this "condition." Excellent reviews of this research have been presented by Friedman (1986) and Risman and Schwartz (1988). One major debate in the research has concerned whether homosexuality is an innate condition or a complex, diffuse experience that anyone may have (Richardson, 1987). Recent writers acknowledge that biological, family, social, and cultural factors all play a role in the development of sexual preference (Marmor, 1980).

Researchers have also investigated the psychological adjustment of individuals with different sexual preferences, demonstrating that gay, lesbian, and bisexual individuals are as healthy as those with a heterosexual preference (Gonsiorek, 1982).

Sociological research in the 1970s shifted to ethnographic study of the gay and lesbian community and the experiences of gay, lesbian, and bisexual individuals both within that community and in interaction with the nongay community (Warren, 1974). The effects of stigma and attitudes about homosexual behavior have also received attention (Watters, 1986).

Gay Identity Development

Recent research has centered on the process by which a gay identity is developed. Like general models of identity development, models outlining gay identity development organize the changes experienced by individuals into stages (Cass, 1983–1984).

Several models of gay identity development have been proposed. Some emphasize the internal psychological process involved (Coleman, 1981–1982; Dank, 1971; Minton and McDonald, 1983–1984; Plummer, 1975; Troiden, 1979). While the number of proposed stages in these models vary, four steps can generally be identified: (1) an increasing acceptance of the homosexual label as applying to one's self, (2) a shift from negative to positive feelings about this self-identity, (3) an increasing desire to inform both gay and nongay individuals of one's gay identity, and (4) more frequent and closer involvement with the gay community.

Other models focus more exclusively on the "coming out" process, that is, the process of identifying as gay both to oneself and to others (DeMonteflores and Schultz, 1978; Hencken and O'Dowd, 1977; Lee, 1977; Lehman, 1978; Moses and Hawkins, 1986). These models suggest a progression that moves from self-acknowledgment, to coming out to significant others, to identifying oneself as gay to the public at large.

A number of researchers have examined factors that influence the coming out process and the development of a gay identity (Hammersmith and Weinberg, 1973; McDonald, 1982; Warren, 1974; Weinberg, 1983). These writers propose that the timing, duration, and outcome of the process are affected by the social context, degree of peer and family support, and psychological adjustment of the individual involved.

While available models have focused our attention on the development of gay identity, a number of weaknesses are apparent (Cass, 1983–1984). Several of the models are purely theoretical, and others are based on research using small samples and poor design. Most of the models are descriptive, failing to discuss how individuals move from one stage to the next and how the cognitive process is different from stage to stage.

The models also assume that the formation of a gay identity is identical for men and women when, in fact, researchers (DeMonteflores and Schultz, 1978; Henderson, 1984; Marmor, 1980) have noted that (1) women tend to develop a lesbian identity later than men develop a gay identity, (2) women tend to develop a lesbian identity before becoming sexually active, (3) emotional attachment is more important than sexual activity to women, (4) homosexuality seems to be less threatening to women than to men, and (5) sexuality tends to be more contextual, relational, and fluid for women than for men. Indeed, Marmor (1980) notes that the experiences of lesbian women are more similar to those of heterosexual women than they are to those of gay men.

Cass (1984) has proposed criteria for a more comprehensive model of gay identity development. They include a clear definition of identity and its relationship to self-concept, an outline of the structural components, changes that occur as identity develops, internal and external factors influencing change, and a clear distinction between cognitive, behavioral, and emotional changes.

Cass's Model of Sexual Identity Formation

Cass (1979b) proposed that homosexual identity is developed through a six-stage process of sexual identity formation that takes into account both psychological and sociological factors. An assumption of the model is that prior to the first stage of development, individuals perceive themselves as heterosexual and nonhomosexual. As these perceptions change, conflict is created between the person's self-perceptions, his or her behavior, and others' perceptions. This conflict either leads toward advancement to a new stage or else results in identity foreclosure. Foreclosure may involve staying at the current stage or moving back to one that was resolved earlier.

The following is a description of the stages in Cass's model. Each stage of the model is characterized by the feelings, behaviors, and beliefs of the individual. For each stage, the predominant conflict is identified and its possible resolution is described.

Stage 1: identity confusion. Stage 1 is entered with the first awareness that some thoughts, feelings, or behaviors might be homosexual in nature. This challenge to one's initial assumptions about sexuality and self-identity lead the individual to question "Who am I?" At this point, it is very rare for someone to self-disclose to others. If the person has acted or acts upon these emerging feelings, conflict is created between his or her self-perceptions and behavior. Resolution of this conflict is strongly shaped by the person's feelings about the desirability and acceptability of the behavior and its meaning. If the person experiences basically positive feelings, movement to Stage 2 occurs.

Stage 2: identity comparison. As congruence between self-perceptions and behavior is achieved, conflict with others' perceptions of the self increases. One of the greatest challenges of stage 2 is dealing with the feelings of social alienation that result from this conflict. The particular methods used to reduce this alienation depend largely on the individual's perceptions of self and behavior. If both are strongly perceived as negative or unacceptable, foreclosure may push the person into a state of denial or self-hatred. If they are seen as acceptable, contact with homosexual others may be initiated, while the person continues to maintain a public image of heterosexuality.

Stage 3: identity tolerance. The individual begins to tolerate a homosexual identity. As the person's private self-image becomes more firmly homosexual, there is increased conflict with the public image. The person may deal with this conflict by seeking out members of and increasing contact with the gay community. The initiation of contact can lead to feelings of increased empowerment as the individual creates new inter- and intrapersonal structures.

Stage 4: identity acceptance. Contacts with the gay or lesbian community serve to validate and "normalize" the individual's homosexual identity. As the person feels increased comfort with his or her identity, conflict arises over outward presentation. This conflict is frequently dealt with through passing, limited contact, or selective disclosure. Passing involves participation in the gay community and the acceptance of a homosexual self-identity while presenting a heterosexual image to the general society. With limited contact, a person severely restricts interactions with those heterosexual others who pose a threat to his or her homosexual identity. In contrast to these two approaches (which serve to avoid conflict), selective disclosure allows an individual to reduce conflict by sharing information about his or her identity with carefully chosen heterosexual individuals. For many, these strategies are effective, and stage 4 becomes a comfortable "place" to stay. If the incongruence remains high, the conflict may push them into stage 5.

Stage 5: identity pride. For individuals in stage 5, conflict between their self-perceptions and others' perceptions of them is at an extremely high level. Strong feelings of frustration and anger with heterosexual society are present, and alienation reemerges. These feelings are often resolved by more severely limiting social contact to the gay or lesbian community, and the individual formulates a dichotomous homosexual (valued) and heterosexual (devalued) world view. Negative responses of heterosexual others serve to confirm and strengthen these perceptions. Positive responses, however, challenge the person's outlook. If the challenge is great, the incongruence may lead to stage 6.

Stage 6: identity synthesis. In the final stage, the individual begins to perceive similarities and dissimilarities with both homosexual and heterosexual others. Although some of the anger and frustration experienced during stage 5 are still present, these feelings are less overwhelming, and the person finds that values may be shared with individual members of both groups. Sexuality is now seen as one part of the total identity, rather than as the main dimension of identity. Although (given the homophobic and heterosexist nature of current society) conflict is never totally eliminated, at stage 6 the incongruence is at its lowest and most manageable point.

While Cass's model presents a clear and integrated picture of sexual identity formation, some limitations exist. Most notable is the breaking down of the identity development process into discrete levels. An inherent weakness in stage models of development is the assumption that development proceeds in a fairly steady, linear progression. In reality, progression through these stages is often marked by movement in both directions. Individuals may also be dealing with issues from more than one stage at a given point, making assignment to a specific stage difficult. However, Cass's work provides both the most comprehensive overview of the homosexual identity development process to date and a strong basis for research in this area.

Impact on College Students

Cass's sexual identity formation (SIF) model describes an identity development process that is full of ambivalence and challenges. Resolution of the issues that arise in the sexual identity formation process requires the focus of a great deal of energy in these areas. For students, these concerns may be at odds with their need to concentrate on issues related to the academic sphere. As pointed out earlier, building self-esteem and developing social skills may be particularly difficult for lesbian and gay college students.

Areas requiring intense concentration, such as mastering new academic skills, may be in competition with the process of working through sexual identity issues. And life goal questions such as career and family plans may be significantly affected by where the student stands in the SIF process.

Levine and Bahr (1989) examined the relationship between SIF and level of psychosocial development. Using a questionnaire based on Cass's (1979a) Stage Allocation Measure and the Student Development Task Inventory-II (SDTI-II) (Winston, Miller, and Prince, 1979), eighty-nine gay and lesbian college students were sampled. For this group, SDTI-II scores dropped through the early and middle SIF stages and then rose in the later SIF stages. In addition, a combination of SIF and academic standing predicted SDTI-II scores, but SDTI-II scores provided no prediction of SIF.

Although sampling students who identified themselves as gay men or lesbian women resulted in a skewing toward later SIF stages (3 through 6), the study sheds some light on the interaction of these two identity development processes. The results suggest that for students in the earlier stages of forging a lesbian or gay identity, resolving sexual identity issues may supersede addressing student development tasks. In addition, the fact that neither SDTI-II nor age predicted SIF indicates that we cannot assume that students of a given age or college year will be in a specific place along the SIF continuum. These findings point to the profound impact of the homosexual identity development process on gay and lesbian students' experiences.

Implications and Future Directions

There is clear indication that the issues with which our gay, lesbian, and bisexual students are dealing are not addressed in traditional student development theory. These identity development issues affect how students perceive themselves and behave in both the academic setting and the world beyond. Student affairs professionals must become more responsive to understanding and meeting the needs of this student group.

There is a need for more research on the impact of sexual identity development on lesbian and gay college students. This research should lead to further refinement of existing identity development models, addressing in particular the nonlinear nature of the identity development process.

In conducting such research, a number of issues need to be considered. Sampling techniques must be carefully evaluated. Techniques that involve gay-identified groups or individuals allow smaller and more easily gathered samples than do more random approaches. However, such techniques virtually eliminate the sampling of students in the earliest levels of the identity development process. In addition, safety issues for participants are paramount. Not only is the maintenance of confidentiality crucial, but also the provision of participant anonymity should be a top priority.

Gender must be considered in future research with gay, lesbian, and bisexual students. Little is known about the differences between gay men and lesbian women in the homosexual identity development process. As is generally true of traditional developmental theories, most models make no gender distinctions in outlining developmental tasks and their resolution (see Chapter Two of this volume). The finding that lesbian women reach awareness of their sexual orientation at a slightly later age than gay men (Moses and Hawkins, 1986) may be reflected in gender ratios of gay/lesbian activity on campuses and provides a challenge to researchers seeking a gender balance in studies with male and female participants.

One last research consideration is the impact of multiple identity development processes. We need to understand how resolution of areas such as gender or racial identity development are juxtaposed with homosexual identity and how these multiple processes relate to student development.

Even in the immediate absence of a large body of research, we must become more active in responding to student needs that are already apparent. Student affairs professionals need to support efforts geared toward empowerment of gay, lesbian, and bisexual students. This support can take many forms.

Proactive measures need to be taken to ensure that our campuses provide a safe environment for our students. Our staffs, both professional and paraprofessional, and student leaders must be educated about and sensitized to the issues of gay, lesbian, and bisexual students. Heterosexual students should also have opportunities to participate in educational programs that demystify homosexuality and increase their comfort with sexuality in general. Institutional policies must clearly provide protection from harassment and discrimination to gay, lesbian, and bisexual students and employees. We must also challenge the heterosexist and homophobic assumptions and values prevalent in our institutional communities.

Lesbian and gay students' fight for recognition of both their existence and needs must have our support and encouragement. Too frequently they are an invisible group on campus, experiencing feelings of being disenfranchised and powerless in the institutional community. Advisers and supporters to individual students and organizations provide role models and help to create a healthy campus environment for these students.

Activities of gay, lesbian, and bisexual students need institutional support and sanctioning. Efforts of clubs and organizations to seek official recognition, to sponsor social events, and to develop support services should receive our full backing. And as we plan programs and events for the campus at large, we must remember and be sensitive to the fact that our audiences include lesbian women and gay men.

This chapter outlines information about homosexuality, the sexual identity formation process, and the needs of our gay, lesbian, and bisexual students. This is only a beginning. In order to be truly responsive to the needs of all students, we must strive toward heightened awareness and advocacy of those students who, in sexual orientation, are pushed outside the mainstream of their campus communities.

References

Adams, J. M. "For Many Gay Teenagers, Torment Leads to Suicide Tries." *Boston Globe,* January 3, 1989, pp. 1–8.

Bell, A. P., and Weinberg, M. S. *Homosexualities: A Study in Diversity Among Men and Women.* New York: Simon & Schuster, 1978.

Bell, A. P., Weinberg, M. S., and Hammersmith, S. K. *Sexual Preference: Its Development in Men and Women.* Bloomington: Indiana University Press, 1981.

Belson, B., and Stamatakos, L. C. *The Student Affairs Profession: A Selective Bibliography.* Washington, D.C.: American College Personnel Association, 1988.

Bendet, P. "Hostile Eyes." *Campus Voice,* Aug.–Sept. 1986, pp. 30–36.

Bourassa, D., and Cullen, M. "Programming: Bringing Gay, Lesbian, and Bisexual Issues to the Forefront." *Profile,* June 1988, pp. 1–6.

Cass, V. C. *Cass Stage Allocation Measure (SAM).* Unpublished manuscript, Doubleview, Australia, 1979a.

Cass, V. C. "Homosexual Identity Formation: A Theoretical Model." *Journal of Homosexuality,* 1979b, *4,* 219–235.

Cass, V. C. "Homosexual Identity: A Concept in Need of Definition." *Journal of Homosexuality,* 1983–1984, *9* (2/3), 105–126.

Cass, V. C. "Homosexual Identity Formation: Testing a Theoretical Model." *Journal of Sex Research,* 1984, *20,* 143–167.

Chickering, A. W. *Education and Identity.* San Francisco: Jossey-Bass, 1969.

Coleman, E. "Developmental Stages of the Coming Out Process." *Journal of Homosexuality,* 1981–1982, *7* (2/3), 31–43.

Dank, B. M. "Coming Out in the Gay World." *Psychiatry,* 1971, *34,* 180–197.

DeMonteflores, C., and Schultz, S. J. "Coming Out: Similarities and Differences for Lesbians and Gay Men." *Journal of Social Issues,* 1978, *34* (3), 59–72.

DeVito, J. A. "Educational Responsibilities to Gay Male and Lesbian Students." In J. W. Chesebro (ed.), *Gayspeak.* New York: Pilgrim Press, 1981.

Erikson, E. H. *Life History and the Historical Moment.* New York: Norton, 1975.

Friedman, R. M. "The Psychoanalytic Model of Male Homosexuality: A Historical and Theoretical Critique." *Psychoanalytic Review,* 1986, *73* (4), 79–115.

Gonsiorek, J. C. "An Introduction to Mental Health Issues and Homosexuality." *American Behavioral Scientist,* 1982, *25,* 367–384.

Hammersmith, S. K., and Weinberg, M. S. "Homosexual Identity: Commitment, Adjustment, and Significant Others." *Sociometry,* 1973, *36,* 56–79.

Hencken, J. D., and O'Dowd, W. T. "Coming Out as an Aspect of Identity Formation." *Gai Saber,* 1977, *1,* 18–22.

Henderson, A. F. "Homosexuality in the College Years: Development Differences Between Men and Women." *Journal of American College Health,* 1984, *32,* 216–219.

Kimmel, D. C. "Adult Development and Aging: A Gay Perspective." *Journal of Social Issues,* 1978, *34* (3), 113–130.

Kinsey, A. C., Pomeroy, W. B., and Martin, C. E. *Sexual Behavior in the Human Male.* Philadelphia: Saunders, 1948.

Kinsey, A. C., Pomeroy, W. B., Martin, C. E., and Beghard, P. H. *Sexual Behavior in the Human Female.* Philadelphia: Saunders, 1953.

Lee, J. A. "Going Public: A Study in the Sociology of Homosexual Liberation." *Journal of Homosexuality,* 1977, *3,* 49–78.
Lehman, L. "What It Means to Love Another Woman." In G. Vida (ed.), *Our Right to Love: A Lesbian Resource Book.* Englewood Cliffs, N.J.: Prentice-Hall, 1978.
Levine, H., and Bahr, J. "Relationship Between Sexual Identity Formation and Student Development." Unpublished manuscript, Philadelphia College of Textiles and Science, Counseling Center, 1989.
Levinson, D. J. *The Seasons of a Man's Life.* New York: Knopf, 1978.
McDonald, G. J. "Individual Differences in the Coming Out Process for Gay Men: Implications for Theoretical Models." *Journal of Homosexuality,* 1982, *8* (1), 47–60.
Marmor, J. "Overview: The Multiple Roots of Homosexual Behavior." In J. Marmor (ed.), *Homosexual Behavior: A Modern Reappraisal.* New York: Basic Books, 1980.
Martin, A. D. "Learning to Hide: The Socialization of the Gay Adolescent." *Psychiatry,* 1982, *10,* 52–63.
Minton, H. L., and McDonald, G. J. "Homosexual Identity Formation as a Developmental Process." *Journal of Homosexuality,* 1983–1984, *9* (2/3), 91–104.
Moses, A. E., and Hawkins, R. O. *Counseling Lesbian Women and Gay Men: A Life Issues Approach.* Columbus, Ohio: Merrill, 1986.
Plummer, K. *Sexual Stigma: An Interactionist Account.* London: Routledge & Kegan Paul, 1975.
Plummer, K. "Building a Sociology of Homosexuality." In K. Plummer (ed.), *The Making of the Modern Homosexual.* Totowa, N.J.: Barnes & Noble, 1981.
Richardson, D. "Recent Challenges to Traditional Assumptions About Homosexuality: Some Implications for Practice." *Journal of Homosexuality,* 1987, *13* (4), 1–12.
Risman, B., and Schwartz, P. "Sociological Research on Male and Female Homosexuality." *Annual Review of Sociology,* 1988, *14,* 125–147.
Scott, D. "Working with Gay and Lesbian Students." *ACU-I Bulletin,* March 1988, pp. 22–25.
Sohier, R. "Homosexual Mutuality: Variation on a Theme by E. Erikson." *Journal of Homosexuality,* 1985–1986, *12* (2), 25–38.
Troiden, R. R. "Becoming Homosexual: A Model of Gay Identity Acquisition." *Psychiatry,* 1979, *42,* 362–373.
Warren, C.A.B. *Identity and Community in the Gay World.* New York: Wiley, 1974.
Watters, A. T. "Heterosexual Bias in Psychological Research on Lesbianism and Male Homosexuality (1977–1983), Utilizing the Bibliographic and Taxonomic System of Morin (1977)." *Journal of Homosexuality,* 1986, *13* (1), 35–58.
Weinberg, T. S. *Gay Men, Gay Selves: The Social Construction of Homosexual Identities.* New York: Irvington, 1983.
Winston, R. B., Jr., Miller, T. K., and Prince, J. S. *The Student Development Task Inventory.* (Rev., 2nd ed.) Athens, Ga.: Student Development Associates, 1979.

Nancy Evans is associate professor of college student personnel at Western Illinois University, Macomb.

Heidi Levine is enrolled in the doctoral program in counseling psychology at Temple University, Philadelphia.

Ethnic influences on student growth and development include differences in attitudes, values, and philosophies of life.

Perspectives on Ethnicity

W. Terrell Jones

In the much quoted *One-Third of a Nation*, a 1988 report by the American Council on Education and the Education Commission of the United States, we are instructed that by the year 2010, one-third of the U.S. population will be regarded as minorities. The compelling nature of this fact is further enhanced by data indicating that, by that same year, 75 percent of all new employees entering the labor market will be either an ethnic minority group member or a female.

The rapid growth and emergence of ethnic groups has challenged the ability of student affairs professionals to effectively serve these new consumers of higher education. Our increasingly heterogeneous student population challenges traditional theories and approaches to student development. If these students are to have equal opportunities to develop to their fullest potential, we must adapt our methods to meet their needs.

The increased cultural diversity of the student population also has implications for how we increase majority students' awareness and appreciation of cultural differences. Through practices, methods, and procedures that do not develop cultural understanding and do not prepare students for the realities of the twenty-first century, student affairs professionals essentially miseducate these students.

Our campuses have always educated those students who best conform to existing campus norms. Although most of our services are standardized on the basis of a homogeneous population and campus environment, that population essentially has disappeared. The homogeneous eighteen- to twenty-two-year-old, middle-class, largely white male college student population is being replaced by one that is increasingly heterogeneous and culturally diverse. This new population demands new insights and shifts in the way we view students and the learning environment. The purpose of this chapter is to specify the types of shifts in perspective needed by campuses as they recast campus norms to accommodate new populations. The chapter includes a description of cultural identity models and five ethnocentric perspectives, and a discussion of the need to revise professional preparation program curricula.

Modifying Our Perspective

When we want to understand people from a culture other than our own, we need to know both about their culture and about how they view themselves in relation to their own culture (Pike, 1967). The terms "etic" and "emic" indicate two approaches to the observer's understanding of other cultures. First used in linguistic science to distinguish speech-sounds (phonetically distinct units of sound) from phonemes (functionally significant units in the sound pattern of a particular language), the concepts connote a separation of general and specific cultural aspects (Pedersen, 1984). The terms have become widely accepted as a distinction between culture-general (etic) and culture-specific (emic) observations. The culture-general observations refer to cultural norms and traditions, and the culture-specific observations are how others view themselves in relation to their culture.

Most traditional theories of individual development do not place such an emphasis on cultural identity. Without this emphasis, developmental theories apply less accurately to ethnic groups. Our current theories fail to address the cultural context and thereby ignore both healthy and unhealthy cultural attitudes held by individuals about their culture. Each person is viewed instead as an autonomous individual who has not been influenced by the cultural norms and values of his or her socialization.

No individual comes to higher education devoid of some influence from his or her culture. The inclusion of cultural identity typologies in our preparation programs and professional development programs will both expand our understanding of new student populations and enhance our ability to exercise leadership in developing an awareness of cultural diversity.

Cultural Identity Models

Understanding how and to what extent an individual is connected to various reference groups is not a new concern. Ho (1987) describes six factors that distinguish ethnic groups as reference groups from middle-class white Americans. Ethnic groups must be viewed in the light of the following factors:

1. The ethnic group's reality: racism and poverty dominate the lives of many ethnic minorities.

2. The impact of external systems on the cultures of the ethnic group: ethnic minority groups experience tensions created by conflicting values between their ethnic culture and white American values.
3. Biculturalism: ethnic minorities are members of two cultural systems, and their level of acculturation to both systems should be considered in understanding them as members of an ethnic group.
4. Ethnicity differences in group's status: historical roots and governmental relationships of a particular ethnic group in the United States indicate or mark the group's status.
5. Ethnicity and language: ethnicity is experienced and persists through language.
6. Ethnicity and social classification: individuals may act in accordance with their perceived class interest in some situations and in accordance with their cultural preferences or ethnic identity in other situations.

Many researchers (Cross, 1971; Vontress, 1981; Helms, 1984; Sue and Sue, 1971; Szapocznik, Kurtines, and Fernandez, 1980), working independently, have developed cultural identity typologies for various ethnic groups. These models are remarkably similar in their description of stage development. They assert the need to understand how ethnic students relate to their own respective cultures and to the culture of the majority. The models also address the coping mechanisms used by ethnic groups to deal with a majority culture that does not value their ethnicity.

In her review of the wide array of models available to explain ethnic identity development, Helms (1985, p. 241) notes that the models seem to have in common the following five assumptions: (1) minority groups develop modal personality patterns in response to white racism; (2) some styles of identity resolution are healthier than others; (3) cultural identity development involves shifts in attitudes involving cognitive, affective, and cognitive components; (4) styles of identity resolution are distinguishable and can be assessed; and (5) intracultural and intercultural interactions are influenced by the manner of cultural identification of the participants.

Minority Identity Development. Of all the models that exist on ethnic identity, the most frequently cited is the minority identity development model (MID). In this model, Atkinson, Morten, and Sue (1983) suggest a five-stage development that is generic for ethnic groups: (1) conformity stage: preference for values of the dominant culture instead of one's own cultural group; (2) dissonance stage: confusion and conflict regarding dominant cultural system and their own group's cultural system; (3) resistance and immersion stage: active rejection of dominant system and acceptance of their own cultural group's traditions and customs; (4) introspection stage: questioning the values of both the minority and the majority cultures; and (5) synergistic articulation and awareness stage: developing a cultural identity that selects elements from both the dominant and minority cultural group values.

Criticism of this model falls into three areas. First, the linear notion of identity is frequently questioned, and there appears to be no clear explanation of just what factors move an individual from one stage to another. Also, the possibility of being in more than one stage as a reaction to different cultural environments is not appropriately addressed. Second, the model is questioned for its underemphasis of Anglo-America's responsibility for the perpetuation of racism (Helms, 1985). Models that "blame the victim" place too much emphasis on the ethnic individual's responses to racism. Helms cautions that an underemphasis of white society's responsibility for the perpetuation of racism encourages an inappropriate focus on changing the ethnic group, as opposed to changing the attitudes and behavior of white society.

The third and more general criticism relates to the lack of models for majority group identity development. While minority group identity has existed for some time, attention to majority group identity has not received the same level of emphasis. This lack of attention may stem from two very different views of identity development. One perspective overemphasizes the attitudes and behavior of highly bigoted whites and does not characterize the identity development of the majority group as a whole. The other perspective is influenced by the belief that the United States is the great "melting pot" and, therefore, should stress cultural similarities rather than differences. By failing to acknowledge differences, the majority culture perpetuates ignorance and ultimately prejudice about differences.

The Emergence of a Majority Group Identity Development Model. Allport (1954) wrote about prejudice. He speculated that roughly four-fifths of North Americans exhibit some identifiable behavior that can be interpreted as antagonistic toward minority groups. Helms (1984) and Bennett (1986) provide a way of analyzing the Allport speculation. Both have developed models of majority member identity development. Both assert that majority group members differ in their awareness and appreciation of cultural diversity and that the ability to perceive cultural differences affects cultural sensitivity. The ability to recognize these differences is the key to providing effective program techniques that are appropriate to the awareness levels of the clientele and thus have a positive impact on cultural sensitivity.

While the Bennett and Helms models of majority member identity development are remarkably similar, the Helms (1984) model is more frequently cited in the literature. This model has the following five stages of white awareness. Helms suggests that a progression through these stages increases racial consciousness and sensitivity.

1. Contact stage: Majority members are only minimally aware of the existence of minority groups and they do not perceive themselves as "racial beings." Differences in cultures and race are minimized and unimportant.

2. Disintegration stage: The majority group members acknowledge that prejudice and discrimination exist. In this stage they are forced to view themselves as majority group members.
3. Reintegration stage: The majority member tends to blame the victims (ethnic group) for creating their own problems.
4. Pseudo-independence stage: The majority member accepts ethnic groups at a conceptual level and becomes interested in understanding racial and cultural differences.
5. Autonomy stage: The individual becomes knowledgeable about racial and cultural similarities and can appreciate all cultures.

Criticism of this and other models of majority cultural awareness are the same as those of ethnic minority models: the model is linear in nature and fails to stress Anglo-American responsibility for perpetuating racism. However, while many of these arguments have some validity, the reader should remember that these models are not social change theories but rather cognitive theories about how individuals make meaning. In this way they are similar to the widely accepted models of Piaget (1970) and Kohlberg (1963).

Ethnocentricity as a Context for Understanding Cultural Differences

This section provides some starting points for understanding Eurocentric, Afrocentric, Sinocentric, Hispanic, and American Indian cultural identities. These frames of reference are simply a place to begin understanding cultural identity and not a hard and fast list of characteristics that can be applied to all members of any cultural group. The reader is again cautioned to approach all cultural investigations from the "emic" perspective that recognizes the tremendous individual differences within each group's frame of reference.

One way to look at ethnic value differences and similarities is through the Kluckhohn and Strodtbeck (1961) model of value orientation. According to Kluckhohn, a value orientation is a generalized and organized concept, influencing our understanding of time, nature, and our place in nature; our relations to other human beings; and the desirable and undesirable aspects of human beings, environments, and interhuman transactions. Ho (1987) has adapted the Kluckhohn and Strodtbeck model to reflect the cultural values of selected ethnic groups and those of middle-class white America. Table 1 provides a comparative summary of the value contrasts associated with Ho's interpretation of the Kluckhohn-Strodtbeck model.

Eurocentric Cultural Identity. For many white Americans the concept of a cultural identity does not exist. These whites have divorced themselves from their own ethnic history, and when questioned about their cultural

Table 1. Cultural Value Preferences of Middle-Class White Americans and Ethnic Minorities

Area of Relationships	*Middle-Class White Americans (Eurocentric)*	*Asian/Pacific Americans (Sinocentric)*	*American Indian*	*African-Americans (Afrocentric)*	*Hispanic-Americans*
Man to nature/ environment	Mastery over	Harmony with	Harmony with	Harmony with	Harmony with
Time orientation	Future	Past-present	Present	Present	Past-present
Relations with people	Individual	Collateral	Collateral	Collateral	Collateral

Note: Adapted from Ho, 1987, p. 232. The value preference called collateral means that people are seen as individuals and also as members of many groups and subgroups; they are independent and dependent at the same time.

heritage, they claim they are "all American" or "a Heinz fifty-seven variety." These statements reflect the still common "melting pot" myth of cultural assimilation. Israel Zangwill (1911), in 1908, introduced the concept of the melting pot in his play, stressing that a new and better culture would grow in the United States as each immigrant gave up old world values for those of the new world. The concept of a melting pot has endured since then. Katz and Ivey (1977) assert that whites who hold the melting pot view and do not see themselves belonging to any race or ethnic group have denied their ethnocentricity and have therefore avoided any responsibility for perpetuating or benefiting from their own ethnic roots.

It is reasonable to assume that whites who deny their own ethnicity will reject ethnic groups who want to stress and celebrate their own cultural uniqueness. Educational pursuits that focus on nonwhite cultures can frustrate white students who deny the value of ethnicity. They continue to believe that everyone could or should assimilate. They are unable to respond with understanding to cultural diversity.

In reviewing Table 1, it is interesting to see how very different the Eurocentric cultural identity is from all others represented in the United States. In the same way, the similarities between other ethnic identities suggest that other groups may be much more able to relate to each other than they can to middle-class white Americans.

Afrocentric Cultural Identity. Most African-Americans are familiar with their dehumanizing history of coming to America and suffering under the institution of slavery, as sanctioned by the designers of our Constitution. The institution of slavery and the psychological by-products of racism, prejudice, and discrimination continue to have a profound, negative impact on all Americans.

In our nation, the most obvious victims of slavery are African-Americans. Throughout their history in this country, they have been forced to project a cultural identity of adaptive inferiority to white society. Some writers (Pugh, 1972; Hayes, 1980) suggest that many of these adaptations were forced on African-Americans by white society. Others (Ellison, 1952; Cheeks, 1976) stress that many of the adaptations were purposeful survival techniques. With the advent of the civil rights movement of the 1960s, a significant, positive change in the collective cultural identity of African-Americans emerged (Jenkins, 1983). The adaptive inferiority was gradually replaced by a greater sense of pride.

This development of a positive cultural identity forms the basis for a healthy self-concept (Poussaint, 1972; Fleming, 1984). A primary source of positive self-concept is family. African-Americans have a historical tradition of organizing the family and extended kinship patterns to provide support and emotional security to family members (Cross, 1978). These patterns reflect their African heritage or Afrocentricity.

Asante (1988) argues that the only way to understand African-Americans is through this Afrocentric philosophy. One must understand not only the cultures and values of Africa but also the philosophies about the nature of human beings and how one should attempt to live. Asante (1988, p. 49) describes a five-level process of developing an Afrocentric perspective: (1) skin recognition: one accepts that his or her skin and cultural heritage are black; (2) environmental recognition: one sees the environment indicting blackness through discrimination and abuse; (3) personality awareness: one begins to accept and view African-American cultural values and traditions as positive; (4) interest concerns: one accepts all the principles of the first three levels and demonstrates concern and interest in the problems of African-Americans; and (5) Afrocentric awareness: one moves to a conscious level of involvement in the struggle for his or her own mind liberation. It is only at this level that the person is aware of the collective conscious will and has the strength to try to eradicate every trace of powerlessness.

Sinocentric Cultural Identity. Asian-American cultural identity is affected by racism, cultural value conflicts, and generational conflicts between parents and children (Sue and Sue, 1985). Asians have a long history as victims of racism and discrimination in the United States, beginning with the Exclusion Act of 1882, which limited Chinese immigration and continues today with refugees from Southeast Asia.

North American whites have a belief that Asians are a model ethnic group. Their belief is based on the stereotype of Asians as hard working, well educated high achievers. While there are some Asians who reflect these attributes, a more critical view of this ethnic group suggests that stereotypes tell only a portion of the story. Asian success rates really are bimodal in that there are highly educated and successful Asians, but there is also another large subgroup characterized by limited education and low income.

Cultural conflict is also a concern. Many Asians must learn to juggle two very different sets of cultural values that seem to directly contradict each other. Americans value independence, autonomy, and individualism, while Asians are much more inclined to value conformity to group, interdependence, and cooperation (see Table 1). What in many cases is perceived by non-Asians as unassertiveness may actually be a manifestation of these cultural contrasts. Weisz, Rothbaum, and Blackburn (1984) emphasize that Asian cultures stress an external locus of control. This preference for external control suggests that Asian-Americans are strongly connected and responsible to family norms and place a high value on cultural continuity.

Asians also face intergenerational differences in value orientation. Chew and Ogi (1987) indicate that there are marked differences between first-, second-, and third-generation adherence to traditional cultural values. First-generation Asians are much more likely to hold traditional Asian values (see Table 1), whereas there seems to be a gradual shift toward traditional, middle-class white North American values for second- and third-generation Asians.

A recent development in many Asian-American communities is the "yellow power movement." As Asians become more aware of discrimination and place a positive emphasis on their own cultural heritage (that is, move into the Atkinson, Morten, and Sue [1983] stage of immersion), activities and groups designed to combat racism will continue to increase. Sue (1981) believes that Asians will become more militant and move toward political action as a change strategy.

Hispanic Cultural Identity. Hispanic-Americans are the fastest growing ethnic group in the United States. "Hispanic" is a term that designates those individuals who live in the United States and whose cultural origins can be traced to Mexico, Puerto Rico, Cuba, and other Latin American countries. Census information indicates that there are over fifteen million Hispanics in the United States. The majority are Mexican-American, followed by Puerto Ricans and Cubans. Hispanics are also the most urbanized ethnic group in North America, with over 85 percent of all Hispanics living in large urban centers (Padilla and DeSnyder, 1985).

In a sense, the term Hispanic does not represent a true ethnic group. The Hispanic culture can trace its origins to Europe, Africa, and Asia (Garcia, 1987). What all Hispanic cultures have in common is that they were at one time Spanish colonies and that Spanish is the dominant language of these cultures. Hispanics face many of the same cultural identity issues that other ethnic groups confront. Like other ethnic groups, they face racism, high unemployment levels, and assimilation.

What separates Hispanics from most other ethnic groups in the United States is that they speak a language other than English in their daily lives (Martinez, 1988). In the case of most ethnic groups, there is a relatively small portion of the group that speaks only their native language. However, in the case of Hispanics and Mexican-Americans in particular, there are still millions who are predominantly Spanish-speaking or bilingual. This language difference suggests that Hispanics are an ethnic group still steeped in its own culture of origin. As a result, the concepts of family, community, religion, and machismo play particularly central roles in defining Hispanic cultural identity. In spite of the size of the Hispanic population in North America, there is still a relatively small literature base characterizing this group.

North American Indian Cultural Identity. North American Indians, including Alaskan natives, are a culturally diverse ethnic group. The 1980 census estimated that there are 1.8 million North American Indians in the United States, with over half the total living in urban communities. Perhaps no other ethnic group in the United States has endured the same persistence of stereotypes as American Indians. As Deloria (1969, p. 45) explains, "People can tell just by looking at us what we want, what should be done to help us, how we feel, and what a 'real' Indian is like."

Throughout the history of whites in North America, Indians have been seen not as victims, but rather as a primitive, hostile culture who had no rights to their lands. Cox (1976) writes that colonialism was responsible for the depreciation of the colored people of the world. In situations where Europeans came upon a people and land they perceived as simple, sparsely populated, and of apparently great exploitive potential, the inhabitants were either eliminated or subjugated. The treatment of the North American Indian fits this pattern.

American Indian cultural identity sharply contrasts with Eurocentric identity. As Ho (1987) notes (see Table 1), Indians have different values with respect to their relationship with nature, time orientation, and other people. American Indians also struggle against a historical pattern of racism and the continuous pressure of assimilation. Over the past two hundred years the federal government has presented Indians with a choice between tribal membership and affiliation versus full assimilation into white society. Many government-sanctioned policies were designed to force the Indians to give up their cultural heritage. Many of these policies still exist. For example, in 1952 the Bureau of Indian Affairs sought to relieve the high level of unemployment by finding jobs for Indians in urban areas and away from their own communities (Stuart, 1977). Programs like this are considered just another attempt by the government to destroy American Indian cultures.

Indian rejection of policies that separate them from their cultures is documented by recent research on American Indian students. Dauphinais, Dauphinais, and Rowe (1981) found that Native American high school students perceived a counselor identified as Native American as more effective than one identified as non-Native American. Scott (1986) found that attachment to Indian culture reduced the chances of academic success. He concludes that in counseling strategies structured to make strongly self-identified Indians "less Indian," these students are likely to choose to drop out of school. Similarly, Johnson and Lashley (1988) note that the degree of Native American cultural commitment (immersion) significantly affected preference for counselor ethnicity. These findings are similar to research on other ethnic group preferences for culture-sensitive educational environments.

Professional Preparation Program Revisions

The wide variety of cultural backgrounds among college students today provides ample support for the need for student affairs professionals to know and understand different cultural perspectives. Historically, however, student personnel and counselor education programs have not been responsive to the needs of ethnic groups (Sue, 1981; Jones, 1987; Pedersen, 1988). While rhetoric stressing the need for multicultural counseling is common in our professional organizations, it usually takes the form of recommendations, endorsements, and guidelines rather than minimal standards for master's-level preparation. In 1986, the Council for the Advancement of Standards for

Student Services/Student Development Programs (CAS) issued a set of standards and guidelines for student affairs master's-level programs (pp. 106–109). While the CAS document is clear in its commitment to ethnic group issues, it fails to include recommendations for acting on that commitment, such as offering courses in multicultural counseling and development as a minimal standard for all master's-level preparation programs.

Student affairs professionals need a systematic way to inform themselves about and to learn to respond to the special concerns of ethnic group students and their increasing impact on the total campus environment. We know the importance of diversity, but, as Hughes (1989) clearly states, while rhetoric on diversity and tolerance abounds, many recent behavioral indicators of the values and attitudes of middle-class white students suggest a different story. The behavioral measures indicate dualistic thinking where the individual views the world in absolutes of right and wrong and cultural differences are seen as deficiencies rather than as alternative world views.

We must all guard against our own monocultural biases in providing services to students. Pedersen (1988), Ho (1987), and Sue (1981) argue that student affairs professionals must face the fact that there is a Western cultural bias in the way they view the world. This bias is not related to our location on the globe, but to our way of thinking about people and things. As professionals, we must realize that most of our psychological theories are Euro-American, founded and standardized on populations that do not reflect the present reality of our campus environments. The results of not examining these biases is cultural encapsulation, which is the raw material that forms racism, homophobia, sexism, ageism, and many other forms of economic and cultural bias (Pedersen, 1988).

As a special note about rainbow coalitions, it is important to recognize that while the frames of reference in this chapter indicate all ethnic groups have been the victims of racism, I do not expect that there will be many coalitions developed between these different groups, even though their value orientations suggest common ground. As Hodgkinson (1987) has speculated, it is possible that the different ethnic groups will find themselves in conflict with each other over resources and group direction. He further states that a rainbow coalition seems to work only when there are specific issues that have a common negative impact on all of the participant ethnic groups.

Summary and Future Implications

Cultural identity will continue to play a dominant role in the lives of ethnic group members. This continued emphasis on ethnicity is also likely to meet with hostility from majority groups. Student affairs professionals must be prepared to meet this new challenge head on. We must design methods and programs that facilitate the social, educational, and cultural awareness of both ethnic and majority students. We need to champion the rights of ethnic groups to explore their own cultural heritage, and we must be ready to provide leadership in resolving intercultural conflicts.

As a predominantly Eurocentric profession, we need first to address our own tendency to perpetuate racism. In order to succeed, we must make it a top priority to acquire multicultural awareness, sensitivity, and intercultural communication skills. Both professional development and new professional preparation programs must adopt this priority. To do less will only serve to keep ethnic groups in the position of victims of racism and ourselves in the role of oppressor.

References

Allport, G. W. *The Nature of Prejudice.* Reading, Mass.: Addison-Wesley, 1954.

American Council on Education. *One-Third of a Nation.* Washington, D.C.: American Council on Education, Education Commission of the United States, 1988.

Asante, M. K. *Afrocentricity.* Trenton, N.J.: Africa World Press, 1988.

Atkinson, D. R., Morten, G., and Sue, D. W. *Counseling American Minorities: A Cross-Cultural Perspective.* (2nd ed.) Dubuque, Iowa: Brown, 1983.

Bennett, M. J. "A Developmental Approach to Training for Intercultural Sensitivity." *International Journal of Intercultural Relations,* 1986, *10* (2), 179–196.

Cheeks, D. K. *Assertive Black . . . Puzzled White.* San Luis Obispo, Calif.: Impact, 1976.

Chew, C. A., and Ogi, A. Y. "Asian American College Students' Perspectives." In D. J. Wright (ed.), *Responding to the Needs of Today's Minority Students.* New Directions for Student Services, no. 38. San Francisco: Jossey-Bass, 1987.

Council for the Advancement of Standards for Student Services/Student Development Programs. *CAS Standards and Guidelines for Student Services/Student Development Programs.* Washington, D.C.: Consortium of Student Affairs Professional Organizations, 1986.

Cox, O. C. *Race Relations Elements and Social Dynamics.* Detroit, Mich.: Wayne State University Press, 1976.

Cross, W. E., Jr. "The Negro-to-Black Conversion Experience: Towards a Psychology of Black Liberation." *Black World,* 1971, *20* (9), 12–37.

Cross, W. E., Jr. "Black Family and Black Identity: A Literature Review." *Western Journal of Black Studies,* 1978, *2,* 111–124.

Dauphinais, P., Dauphinais, L., and Rowe, W. "Effects of Race and Communication Style on Indian Perceptions of Counselor Effectiveness." *Counselor Education and Supervision,* 1981, *21,* 72–80.

Deloria, V., Jr. *Custer Died for Your Sins: An Indian Manifesto.* New York: Macmillan, 1969.

Ellison, R. *Invisible Man.* New York: Signet Books, 1952.

Fleming, J. *Blacks in College: A Comparative Study of Students' Success in Black and White Institutions.* San Francisco: Jossey-Bass, 1984.

Garcia, E.L.Q. "Facilitating the Development of Hispanic College Students." In D. J. Wright (ed.), *Responding to the Needs of Today's Minority Students.* New Directions for Student Services, no. 38. San Francisco: Jossey-Bass, 1987.

Hayes, W. A. "Radical Black Behaviorism." In R. L. Jones (ed.), *Black Psychology.* (2nd ed.) New York: Harper & Row, 1980.

Helms, J. E. "Toward a Theoretical Explanation of the Effects of Race on Counseling: A Black and White Model." *Counseling Psychologist*, 1984, *12* (4), 153–164.
Helms, J. E. "Cultural Identity in the Treatment Process." In P. Pederson (ed.), *Handbook of Cross-Cultural Counseling and Therapy*. Westport, Conn.: Greenwood, 1985.
Ho, M. K. *Family Therapy with Ethnic Minorities*. Newbury Park, Calif.: Sage, 1987.
Hodgkinson, H. L. "The Demographic Picture and What It Means for Higher Education: Special Report." *Black Issues in Higher Education*, 1987, *3* (22), 2–3.
Hughes, M. "A Time to Speak." *ACPA Developments* (Newsletter of the American College Personnel Association), 1989, *16* (3), 188.
Jenkins, A. *The Psychology of the Afro-American*. Elmsford, N.Y.: Pergamon Press, 1983.
Johnson, M. E., and Lashley, K. H. "Influence of Native-Americans' Cultural Commitment on Preference for Counselor Ethnicity." *Journal of Multicultural Counseling and Development*, 1988, *17* (30), 115–122.
Jones, W. T. "Enhancing Minority-White Peer Interaction." In D. J. Wright (ed.), *Responding to the Needs of Today's Minority Students*. New Directions for Student Services, no. 38. San Francisco: Jossey-Bass, 1987.
Katz, J. H., and Ivey, A. "White Awareness: The Frontier of Racism Awareness Training." *Personnel and Guidance Journal*, 1977, *55*, 485–487.
Kluckhohn, F. R., and Strodtbeck, F. L. *Variations in Value Orientations*. New York: Harper & Row, 1961.
Kohlberg, L. "Moral Development and Identification." In H. Stevenson (ed.), *Child Psychology. 62nd Yearbook of the National Society for the Study of Education*. Part 1. Chicago: University of Chicago Press, 1963.
Martinez, C. "Mexican Americans." In L. Comas-Diaz and E.E.H. Griffith (eds.), *Cross-Cultural Mental Health*. New York: Wiley, 1988.
Padilla, A. M., and DeSnyder, N. S. "Counseling Hispanics: Strategies for Effective Intervention." In P. Pedersen (ed.), *Handbook of Cross-Cultural Counseling and Therapy*. Westport, Conn.: Greenwood Press, 1985.
Pedersen, P. "Introduction: The Cultural Complexity of Mental Health." In P. Pedersen, N. Sartorius, and A. J. Marsella (eds.), *Mental Health Services: The Cross-Cultural Context*. Newbury Park, Calif.: Sage, 1984.
Pedersen, P. *A Handbook for Developing Multicultural Awareness*. Alexandria, Va.: American Association for Counseling and Development, 1988.
Piaget, J. *Structuralism*. New York: Basic Books, 1970.
Pike, K. L. *Language in Relation to a United Theory of the Structure of Human Behavior*. The Hague, The Netherlands: Mouton, 1967.
Poussaint, A. F. *Why Blacks Kill Blacks*. New York: Emerson Hall, 1972.
Pugh, R. W. *Psychology and the Black Experience*. Monterey, Calif.: Brooks/Cole, 1972.
Scott, W. J. "Attachment to Indian Culture and the 'Difficult Situation': A Study of American Indian College Students." *Youth and Society*, 1986, *17* (4), 381–395.
Stuart, P. "United States Indian Policy." *Social Service Review*, 1977, *47*, 451–463.
Sue, D. W. *Counseling the Culturally Different*. New York: Wiley-Interscience, 1981.
Sue, W. S., and Sue, D. W. "Chinese-American Personality and Mental Health." *Amerasia Journal*, 1971, *1*, 36–49.
Sue, W. S., and Sue, D. W. "Asian-Americans and Pacific Islanders." In P. Pedersen (ed.), *Handbook of Cross-Cultural Counseling and Therapy*. Westport, Conn.: Greenwood Press, 1985.
Szapocznik, J., Kurtines, W. M., and Fernandez, T. "Bicultural Involvement and Adjustment in Hispanic-American Youths." *International Journal of Intercultural Relations*, 1980, *4*, 353–365.

Vontress, C. E. "Racial Differences: Impediments to Rapport." *Journal of Counseling Psychology,* 1981, *18,* 7-13.

Weisz, R. R., Rothbaum, F. M., and Blackburn, T. C. "Standing Out and Standing In: The Psychology of Control in America and Japan." *American Psychologist,* 1984, *39* (9), 955-969.

Zangwill, I. *The Melting-Pot, Drama in Four Acts.* New York: Macmillan, 1911.

W. Terrell Jones is special assistant to the provost for underrepresented groups and affiliate assistant professor of counselor education at The Pennsylvania State University, University Park.

Students' interactions with their environments are influenced by their ethnocentric perspectives, by their views of themselves as members of oppressed or oppressing groups, and by the cultural values of the campus.

Applying Cultural Theory: The Environmental Variable

Paul Shang, Leila V. Moore

Theories about the campus environment and how students react to it confirm the importance of positive interaction with one's environment as a significant variable in student growth. The historical roots of environmental theory can probably be traced to Lewin's (1936) formulation: behavior is a function of the interaction of certain personal characteristics with certain environmental characteristics. The development of this principle as it relates to the collegiate environment was triggered by the writings of the Western Interstate Commission for Higher Education (WICHE) (WICHE, 1973; Aulepp and Delworth, 1976). WICHE researchers introduced the idea that the campus environment, the organizational structure of the institution, the needs of all members of the campus community, and the members' perceptions of the environment must fit together in a compatible ecosystem in order to optimize the growth and well-being of those who work and study on campus.

These concepts about managing the campus environment took hold quickly on college campuses. Good person-environment "fits" were reported as a factor in student retention (Astin, 1975), in positive growth experiences for students (Holahan and Wilcox, 1977; Moos, 1976), and in the principles of assessment (Aulepp and Delworth, 1978).

As social climate and environment continued to be a focus of energy for college administrators, the notion of "chilly" climates emerged. Our first understanding of the term chilly climate emerged from discussion of women's needs and rights on campus. In Chapter Two, Kuk points out that higher education's traditional focus on white males and the absence of women from the theoretical base of human development contribute to the current "chilly" atmosphere endured by women on college campuses.

The Western European cultural bias evident in human development theories and the problem of how this bias prevents student affairs professionals from creating an inclusive environment responsive to the needs of all students are explored by Jones in Chapter Five. Within the context of the climate of hostility experienced by gay, lesbian, and bisexual students on college campuses, Evans and Levine describe in Chapter Four the further limitations of developmental theory resulting from the theoretical presumption of heterosexuality.

As campus populations have become increasingly diverse, there is a corresponding need to develop a campus environment that responds to diversity. The person-environment theories may be stretched to their limits as they are used in conjunction with the goal of inclusion of all co-cultures on our campuses. The value of inclusion will be difficult to introduce, however, as many campuses still experience the domination by one co-culture of all other co-cultures.

Hilliard (1986) argues that the following steps are among those taken when one group attempts to dominate another group: (1) suppression of the history of a dominated group, (2) suppression of cultural forms of a dominated group, (3) suppression of group identity for members of a dominated group, and (4) teaching the superiority of the dominating group. From the perspective of minority peoples, institutions of higher education may represent the culmination of these steps of oppression. With regard to minority students and students from economically disadvantaged backgrounds, colleges and universities may represent the last educational opportunity to impose the "political and ideological use of the cultural deprivation hypothesis" (Ryan, 1971, pp. 31–32), which rejects inherent inferiority but insidiously substitutes functional inferiority in its place. However difficult it may be to foster inclusivity, many institutions have begun to incorporate the needs and the contributions of those historically left out by traditional approaches.

Institutions of higher education have taken steps to modify the effects on their campuses of institutional racism, sexism, and other "isms." Much more can be done to make the college experience more inclusive of the perspectives and values of all participants. The campus environment must reflect a greater awareness of the contributions made by African-American, Hispanic-American, Asian-American, and American Indian students and the conditions under which people of color live and are educated in this society.

The dialogue concerning how best to serve a multicultural, multiethnic student body is often confusing in academic settings, even when all acknowledge the immediacy of the need. Part of the reasons for this confusion has to do with the slippery nature of the language used. For instance, what is meant by the term "culture"? The anthropologist E. B. Tylor, the first to use the term in English as a scientific term, defined culture and civilization as "that complex whole which includes knowledge, belief, art, morals, law, custom, and any other capabilities and habits" that are obtained as a member of society (1903, vol. 1, p. 1). Current understandings of the term are equally as broad.

As with the notion of culture, the idea of ethnicity is also general. What is conveyed by ethnicity is a sense of what a group of people have in common, perpetuated over time by the family and sustained by the community (McGoldrick, 1982, p. 4). Ethnicity goes beyond national origin, religion, or even race in providing an enduring sense of identity and belonging to a group of people.

What is meant by race is also subject to dispute. As discussed in UNESCO's *Statement of 1950,* the people of the world can be divided into three major groups: Caucasian, Negroid, and Mongoloid. Each division has different subgroups (UNESCO, 1969, pp. 497–498). These races can be differentiated by the color of the skin, the feel and color of the hair, bodily proportions, and other similar physical and hereditary characteristics. In the United States, then, each of the three main races are amply represented.

Rapid Change, Cultural Diversity, and Environmental Resistance

On many campuses, cultural diversity among student enrollments has been a fairly sudden change. From fall 1976 to fall 1982, for example, the number of white students enrolled in colleges and universities increased by a little more than 5 percent (305,000) compared to a more than 15 percent increase (140,000) of minority students during the same time period (Arbeiter, 1986, p. 3). At some of this country's more prominent institutions of higher education, African-American, Hispanic-American, Asian-American, and American Indian students now comprise a sizeable portion of the student body. For instance, at the University of California, Los Angeles, 62 percent of the 1988 freshman class is minorities, as is almost 50 percent of all undergraduate students (Mooney, 1988, p. A11); at the University of Michigan over 20 percent of the entering freshmen is minorities while over 15 percent of the student body is minorities; and at Vanderbilt, with a total minority population of over 8 percent, almost 11 percent of the recent freshmen class is minority students (Magner, 1988, p. A26).

It seems tempting to conclude that these numerical increases signal a significant erosion of traditional institutional barriers to the enrollment of ethnic minority students. While this may be partially true, the daily experiences of minority students attending predominantly white colleges and universities underscore a general institutional ambivalence toward their educational needs, a lack of appreciation for their cultural heritages, and callousness toward values other than the prevalent ones. More African-American, Hispanic-American, Asian-American, and American Indian students are participating in higher education. By some estimates, however, only 42 percent of African-American students entering college and 31.3 percent of Hispanic-American students will eventually graduate (Astin, 1982, p. 41). Even fewer minority students will earn advanced degrees, and as many as 25 percent will experience some form of racially motivated attack during an academic year (Selinker, 1988).

Higher education has had a difficult time addressing perspectives rooted in the cultural heritage of individual students. Much of the effort directed toward assisting minority students to succeed at colleges and universities focuses on improving skills, providing an orientation to a new environment, and attempting to compensate somehow for the economic status of their backgrounds. These students, regardless of how they might perceive themselves, are categorized frequently as academic underachievers, "high risk," or from disadvantaged backgrounds. What still seems to be missing is an institutional understanding that these labels still illustrate theories of oppression and indicate a poor "fit" between the campus environment and the needs of the students.

Within-Group Cultural Diversity

Another primary difficulty of developing the institutional value of inclusivity is the persistent stereotyping of individuals based on what is believed to be their cultural, ethnic, or racial backgrounds. However, one's cultural background does not affect all members in the same way. Depending on their individual experiences, people's ethnic and cultural identities may demonstrate greater or lesser degrees of acculturation or assimilation. For instance, an Asian-American whose family has lived in this country for several generations may speak English as a first language, may not understand an Asian language at all, may marry out of the ethnic group, and may not have grown up in an Asian-American community. For an Asian-American whose family has recently immigrated and lives in an Asian-American community, the cultural experience and the degree of ethnic identity may be quite different. Yet, both will have some similar experiences as well because of their race and the way others respond to their race. Just as African-Americans from the rural South, the inner city, and the middle-class suburbs may have significantly different cultural experiences, they also share similar experiences because of how others relate to them racially.

Another variable that affects diversity within a racial or ethnic group is economic class. Economic well-being permits the enjoyment of opportunities for a quality education and many other advantages that are important in an individual's life experience. However, economic conditions can also be such that some groups, such as whites in southern Appalachia or white Cajuns in Louisiana who have been unable to advance into the middle class, identify more with the cultural motifs of some minority groups (Anderson, 1988, p. 3).

The population of Asian-Americans contains an example of diversity in values about economic stability. During the 1970s and 1980s the enrollment of Asian-Americans in colleges and universities increased dramatically. Observers have commented on the prevalence of Asian-American students in the applied sciences and have attributed this phenomenon to their desire to find occupations that avoid conflict with the group identity and cultural values of reserve and propriety ("Asian Students Prefer Science . . . ," 1987). While there is probably some truth to this explanation, it should be remembered that unlike previous immigrants from Europe, Asian immigrants come mainly from the educated middle class and, except for the Southeast Asian refugees, are at least twice as likely to have a college degree as someone born in the United States (Doerner, 1985, p. 43). Since the reform of the immigration laws in 1965, Asians have been arriving at such a high rate that they are this country's fastest growing ethnic minority group. In addition to their own cultural values, the new Asian immigrants are also motivated by the general immigrant ethic to achieve economic stability for their families as quickly as possible.

Differences in Values About Education

Cultural heritage affects education. In seeking to understand this principle, it is beneficial to turn to experiences of colleagues in elementary and secondary education.

For instance, student conduct problems arising from the inability of authority figures such as teachers to impose their control may be more obvious with elementary and high school age students. On the college level, where the classroom atmosphere is informal and faculty strive to create an egalitarian atmosphere, students accustomed to a more direct imposition of authority may not recognize the rules of the game and thus may fail to understand what degree of compliance is really expected at the college level. In the African-American community authoritative teachers are able to communicate their personal power, establish positive relationships with students, compel students to reach a standard of achievement clearly determined by the teacher, and interact with students in mutually familiar ways (Delpit, 1988, p. 290). These attitudes toward authority, while widely held by people of certain cultures or economic classes, are not usually accommodated by the teaching practices current in higher education.

Another example of culturally based values conflicting with the middle-class white values prevalent in higher education is provided by the experience of American Indian students. In American Indian culture cooperation within the group is highly valued, whereas competition is not encouraged (Mitchum, 1989, p. 267). Higher education, in contrast, encourages competition and asks individuals to distinguish themselves from the group through their own achievements. The problem with using competition and individual accomplishments as teaching tools is that for those students whose cultures do not recognize these values, the tools can become impediments to learning.

Finally, the value on getting an education varies widely. For some students, education is a necessity, a foregone conclusion. But for others, minority students and other students from economically poor families, there are feelings of guilt about being the recipients of the luxury of attending college. Despite potentially dire personal results, these students are likely to deplete their limited financial aid awards by sending money home to support their families.

Cultural Experiences as Unique Variables in Retention

In the context of providing admissions opportunities to a broad range of students, some researchers have maintained that attitudes and cultural experiences occurring prior to college are more predictive of success for minority students than the more widely used standardized instruments such as the College Board's Scholastic Aptitude Test (SAT). One such measure of student experiences before college is the Noncognitive Questionnaire (NCQ). The NCQ evaluates noncognitive dimensions, including whether or not the student possesses a positive self-image, is realistic about his or her academic skills, understands and is able to cope with racism, is able to work toward long-range goals at the expense of short-range goals, has available support systems, has had leadership experience, has been involved with the community, and has extracurricular interests associated with academic subjects (Tracey and Sedlacek, 1985, p. 406).

According to Tracey and Sedlacek (1985), variables measured by the NCQ predict the continued enrollment of African-American students much better than their SAT scores. Another precollege factor for African-American students that seems to have a positive effect on college experiences is positive interracial contact. For both males and females, African-American students who had positive interracial contacts prior to college enjoyed positive interracial contacts at college, were more accepting of ethnic diversity, and felt less alienated from the campus community (Bennett, 1984; Bennett and Okinaka, 1984). These students also tended to be more satisfied with college life and had a stronger commitment to complete their degrees than African-American students without such positive prior experience.

Curriculum Changes Recognizing Cultural Diversity

Colleges and universities have begun to make changes in their curricula to educate students about the contributions of minorities and women and to prepare students for life in a multicultural society. Two such changes are occurring at Stanford University and at the University of California,

Berkeley. These changes are prototypes for what other colleges and universities will adopt eventually in order to address the needs of students and to provide a more adequate background for understanding the different cultural traditions within the society.

In the case of Stanford, the Faculty Senate recently decided to replace the Western Culture requirement with a year-long program called "Cultures, Ideas, and Values." As a result, more discussion of issues having to do with race, gender, and class as well as greater focus on the contributions of women and members of minority groups will be incorporated into each related course (Mooney, 1988). Students at Stanford will be required to study works from at least one other culture in order to supplement the ideas originating in European, ancient, and medieval cultures.

Similarly, at the University of California, Berkeley, faculty have approved a one-course "American Cultures" requirement, emphasizing the country's multicultural heritage. Beginning in 1991, students must study works from three American cultural groups, including African-Americans, American Indians, Asian-Americans, Chicano/Latinos, and European-Americans as part of the graduation requirement (McNulty, 1989).

Each institution in its own way has made significant changes in order to highlight the multicultural heritage of this country and to expand the notion of Western culture to incorporate the contributions, traditionally not mentioned, made by women and members of minority groups. These changes have come with controversy. In the minds of some students, faculty, and staff, the changes represent an assault on academic quality and integrity and a denigration of the accomplishments of Western culture. To others, a full appreciation of similarities can only come through the recognition of different life experiences and the legitimization of everyone's contributions.

The ethnic and cultural composition of American society is undergoing dramatic and rapid change. According to current projections, by 2020 more than one out of every three Americans will be a person of color. In order to meet future challenges, it is incumbent on higher education in the United States to learn how to serve students from different cultural backgrounds. As discussed here, the past thirty years for higher education has been a period where questions concerning the relationship of cultural heritage and educational experiences have come to the forefront. Undeniably, there have been bold initiatives that not only recognize the contributions made by women and members of minority groups but also insist that well-educated students should be aware of these contributions and of their impact. Because higher education trains future political and business leaders, educators, and professionals, it must assume a leadership role in response to the pressing social need of preparing people for life and work in a multicultural society.

The question of how to best accomplish this task is difficult to answer. Even with the diversity of students present, the educational experiences taking place on college campuses are somewhat removed from the surrounding communities. For most colleges and universities, even the minority students in attendance are already members of elite groups. While the high school graduation rate for African-American students has risen to almost 60 percent in 1983, the proportion of African-American high school graduates who go on to college has declined to only 38.5 percent; similarly, while about 50 percent of Hispanic-American students graduate from high school, only 46.5 percent of Hispanic-American high school graduates enrolled in college in 1983 (Arbeiter, 1986, p. 4). As the recent experiences at Stanford and Berkeley have shown, to effectively teach the new multicultural curricula, faculty at institutions of higher education must become more familiar with the experiences and the contributions of members of the different minority groups. In doing so, they must not only alter the classroom environment to be more inclusive but also reform their institution's value system to adopt the value of inclusivity.

Endnotes and a Bridge to the Future

Our history in the formulation and use of theory has its roots in a Eurocentric perspective. As we initiated our reliance on theory, we drew exclusively from male theorists who wrote from this particular perspective and tested their theories on a predominantly white, male student population. It is not surprising to see that in the last several years, challenges to existing theories have come from other ethnocentric perspectives, from those concerned about campus populations who do not "fit" these theories, and largely from writers who are not white males.

Our changing campus populations have finally focused our attention on the need for new theories and models. We have turned to the disciplines of anthropology and sociology for more information about ethnocentric perspectives. We are gradually getting used to the idea that our research methodologies must include qualitative approaches.

Even our language about the use of theory is changing. We hear about and study nonlinear models. For example, we recognize that growth can be explained more often with "chaoticdynamics" (Caple, 1989) than it can through a straight line progression. We see greater relevance of theories that discuss movement from simple to more complex levels of understanding. In short, we are moving toward a multiplicity of perspectives in our theory base.

As we expand our view beyond its origins in a Eurocentric perspective, though, we seem to be unaware of how very different this perspective is from nearly all other ethnocentric perspectives (see Chapter Five). It is not really surprising to see conflict result when students from diverse cultures and ethnic backgrounds arrive on a college campus that is Eurocentric in its ethnicity, culture, and traditions. The cultural clashes are frequent and sometimes violent.

As educators in this climate, we witness these conflicts and attempt to mediate, manage, and resolve. Unfortunately, we intervene from assumptions of adaptation and assimilation. Rarely do we modify our view that we are the teacher (the one who does not need to change any more), and the student is the one to be educated or changed. Rarely do we modify our campus culture by challenging long-standing traditions or by causing other basic changes in the Eurocentric campus culture. We are slow to challenge the Eurocentric values that underpin institutional mission, policies, and priorities. Paradoxically, we use an existing theory base that describes changes within students, but we do not see that these same theories must also apply to change within us and within our social environments.

References

Anderson, J. A. "Cognitive Styles and Multicultural Populations." *Teacher Education,* 1988, *39* (1), 2-9.

Arbeiter, S. "Minority Enrollment in Higher Education Institutions: A Chronological View." In *Research and Development Update.* New York: College Entrance Examination Board, 1986.

"Asian Students Prefer Science for Cultural Reasons, Researchers Say." *Equal Opportunity in Higher Education,* March 12, 1987, p. 8.

Astin, A. W. *Preventing Students from Dropping Out: A Multi-Institutional Study of College Dropouts.* San Francisco: Jossey-Bass, 1975.

Astin, A. W. *Minorities in American Higher Education: Recent Trends, Current Prospects, and Recommendations.* San Francisco: Jossey-Bass, 1982.

Aulepp, L., and Delworth, U. *Training Manual for an Ecosystem Model: Assessing and Designing Campus Environments.* Boulder, Colo.: Western Interstate Commission for Higher Education, 1976.

Aulepp, L., and Delworth, U. "A Team Approach to Environmental Assessment." In J. H. Banning (ed.), *Campus Ecology: A Perspective for Student Affairs.* Cincinnati, Ohio: National Association of Student Personnel Administrators, 1978.

Bennett, C. "Interracial Contact Experience and Attrition Among Black Undergraduates at a Predominantly White University." *Theory and Research in Social Education,* 1984, *12* (2), 19-47.

Bennett, C., and Okinaka, A. "Explanations of Black Student Attrition in Predominantly White and Predominantly Black Universities." *Integrateducation,* 1984, 22 (1-3), 73-80.

Caple, R. B. "Editorial." *Journal of College Student Development,* 1989, *30* (4), 291-292.

Delpit, L. D. "The Silenced Dialogue: Power and Pedagogy in Educating Other People's Children." *Harvard Educational Review,* 1988, *58* (3), 280-288.

Doerner, W. R. "Asians: To America with Skills." *Time,* July 8, 1985, pp. 42-44.

Hilliard, A. G. "The Theoretical and Historical Bases for Multicultural Counseling and Psychotherapy." Keynote address at the American Association for Counseling and Development Symposium on Multicultural Counseling, Atlanta, Ga., February 28-March 2, 1986.

Holahan, C. J., and Wilcox, B. L. "Ecological Strategies in Community Psychology: A Case Study." *American Journal of Community Psychology,* 1977, *5* (4), 423-433.

Lewin, K. *Principles of Topological Psychology.* New York: McGraw-Hill, 1936.

McGoldrick, M. "Ethnicity and Family Therapy: An Overview." In M. McGoldrick, J. K. Pearce, and J. Giordano (eds.), *Ethnicity and Family Therapy.* New York: Guilford, 1982.

McNulty, J. "Berkeley Faculty Approves Controversial Ethnic Studies Requirement." *Black Issues in Higher Education,* 1989, *6* (6), 14.

Magner, D. K. "Enrollment Rises on Some Campuses Due to Intensified Recruiting Efforts." *Chronicle of Higher Education,* December 14, 1988, p. A26.

Mitchum, N. T. "Increasing Self-Esteem in Native-American Children." *Elementary School Guidance & Counseling,* 1989, *23* (4), 266–271.

Mooney, C. J. "Sweeping Curricular Change Is Underway at Stanford as University Phases Out Its 'Western Culture' Program." *Chronicle of Higher Education,* December 14, 1988, pp. A1, A11–A13.

Moos, R. H. *The Human Context: Environmental Determinants of Behavior.* New York: Wiley-Interscience, 1976.

Ryan, W. *Blaming the Victim.* New York: Vintage, 1971.

Selinker, M. "Revival of Overt Racism Plagues Colleges." *U.: The National College Newspaper,* 1988, *1,* 1–2.

Tracey, T. J., and Sedlacek, W. E. "The Relationship of Noncognitive Variables to Academic Success: A Longitudinal Comparison by Race." *Journal of College Student Personnel,* 1985, *26* (5), 405–410.

Tylor, E. B. *Primitive Culture: Researches into the Development of Mythology, Philosophy, Religion, Language, Art, and Custom.* 2 vols. (4th ed.) London: John Murray, 1903.

UNESCO. *Statement of 1950: Race and Science.* New York: Columbia University Press, 1969.

Western Interstate Commission for Higher Education. *The Ecosystem Model: Designing Campus Environments.* Boulder, Colo.: Western Interstate Commission for Higher Education, 1983.

Paul Shang is director of the Help for Education and Life Planning Success Center at Colorado State University, Fort Collins.

Leila V. Moore is with the Division of Student Programs at The Pennsylvania State University, University Park. She is also president-elect of the American College Personnel Association. Both authors are trainers for the American College Personnel Association's National Workshops on Cultural Diversity.

Emerging developmental theories have implications for student affairs practice now and in the future.

Student Development: Yesterday, Today, and Tomorrow

Robert D. Brown, Margaret J. Barr

Student affairs and college student development theories have been traveling companions for many years. For us, Nevitt Sanford's (1962) *The American College* represents a significant milestone of this friendship. Like our colleagues in child and adult development, the professionals in college student affairs find that developmental theories provide useful frameworks for understanding students, establishing program goals, and determining program activities. Stage theories provide residence education staff with insights and topics for floor or hall programs that focus on developmental issues students face as they enter college, make career choices, and cope with crises relating to intimacy. Developmental domains provide target goals (for example, Chickering's [1969] vectors such as autonomy and sense of purpose) for campus activity coordinators working with student leaders. Breaking developmental goals into specific tasks improves program evaluators' chances of assessing student growth (see Winston and Miller, 1987). The theoretical perspectives provide practitioners with a rationale and framework for their practice, and the results of in-the-field research on college campuses provide researchers with an avenue for testing the application of the theories.

But like good friends, student affairs professionals and student development theorists also risk becoming each other's worst enemies. Blind acceptance can lead to misunderstandings. The relationship can be taken for granted, grow stale, and eventually end. Rival conceptualizations of what the profession is about may appear fresher and at first glance more salient to the everyday work of the practitioner. Theorists and researchers may wish to make their mark by advocating more novel theories to test.

Certainly, this would not be a new phenomenon in the history of science or of practice. The friendship between student affairs professionals and student development theorists is at that critical point now, which is why this volume is important. The excitement of the initial discoveries has worn thin, overgeneralizations have led to misapplication, and what once seemed like a perfect match now is something that clearly demands solid rethinking and hard work.

In this chapter, we discuss the implications for practice by identifying barriers for translating theory to practice and by sharing our biases with you. In addition, we provide some examples of applied theory in the daily work of student affairs and identify methods to aid in the translation process. Finally, we identify what we believe to be the agenda for the future as we struggle to learn more about our students.

Implications for Practice

What do all of the emerging theoretical perspectives actually mean for student affairs practitioners? For many, discussions of developmental theory are interesting and often challenging, but a translation is not made into the daily work of the practice. Why is that so?

Barriers to Translation. Several barriers are present in the process of translating theory to practice. First, there is a lack of shared understanding about developmental theory. Within a student affairs division, the level of understanding of developmental constructs varies widely. This often relates to the many and diverse academic backgrounds of student affairs staff. Many staff have not been exposed to developmental theories prior to employment in student affairs. The issue is further complicated when a developmental perspective is not clearly articulated within the division of student affairs and the institution. Under those conditions, opportunities for collaboration are meager and motivation for testing and applying theory is diminished.

Second, new theoretical perspectives and models, such as those described in this volume, are rarely discussed in an explicit way by most practitioners. Lack of information may result in application of theories in an inappropriate way to specific subpopulations. When that occurs, failure often is the result, and the use of theory as a tool is abandoned.

Third, in some professional settings, concerted effort is not given to making theory a useful tool for practice. There is a "so what?" attitude that pervades the organization. As a result, policies, programs, practices, and procedures continue without examination of the potential effect they may have on certain students. Hurst and Jacobson (1985) describe this approach to student affairs as one where the student must adjust to the institution rather than the institution adjust to the student.

Fourth, a lack of understanding of the major function of theory persists and creates a formidable barrier for applied theory. Hoy and Miskel (1978, p. 21) identify the major function of theory as a tool "to describe, explain, and predict behavior." If theory remains in a category of interesting information rather than an active means to guide practice, it is of little use.

Finally, some practitioners view theory in a unidimensional fashion. A developmental theory is adopted and used to guide practice with all students. Such exclusive adherence to one theoretical perspective blinds professionals to subtle but important differences among students. A narrow view of developmental theory becomes a limiting factor rather than a means to broaden the base of understanding and improve programs and services.

A Bias. It is important to acknowledge a bias reflected in this chapter. We believe that developmental theory provides a unique perspective on all aspects of our work (Brown, 1972). Much as an artist views the world using form and color, the student affairs professional who has a developmental perspective usually approaches tasks in a way different from that of the professional who lacks such a perspective. The whole person is considered and both the "how" and the "why" of each task are considered. Many of the responsibilities of student affairs professionals can be approached either from a task orientation or from a perspective that pays attention to both task and process. For example, career planning and placement offices routinely schedule orientation sessions for senior students who are about to enter the interview process. The most efficient way to schedule these sessions is in a large group where the representative of career planning and placement outlines procedures and forms are distributed. The question-and-answer period is conducted in a large group and then the students are dismissed. If this same task is approached from a developmental perspective, staff members recognize that all students are not equally prepared to enter into the interview process. Further, they recognize that anxieties may be high, that students have received conflicting advice, and that some students are very confused. With these understandings in mind, the senior orientation is conducted in an entirely different manner. While information may still be given in a large group, questions and answers are handled in a small group format. Specific instructions are given in writing, and follow-up sessions on interviewing skills and resumé writing are already scheduled. Students encountering difficulty are immediately signed up for one of these groups. The small group also gives students and staff an opportunity to become acquainted and for students to identify an individual that they can call on if they encounter difficulty. The task and objectives for senior placement orientation remain the same, but the processes are markedly different. The emerging theoretical perspectives described in this volume also have similar potential for influencing professional practice.

Applications. The work of Cross (1978) and others provides significant help for student affairs professionals who implement programs and services directed toward minority students. We are reminded that all minority students are not alike, nor are they all in the same stage of development. This theoretical perspective reaffirms the need for ethnic minority support groups, recognition, and celebration of events such as National Hispanic Week and Martin Luther King's birthday while understanding that such events may not be equally supported by all minority students. It also broadens our understanding of the differences among students. For example, there may be great differences in the way a new minority freshman wants and needs to interact with the majority culture compared to a junior or senior who has become immersed in the minority culture. Relationships between students that have been easy may become difficult. Involvement patterns may change and relationships with those in authority may be altered. Although such understanding may not always ease our discomfort, it does help us to explain and predict behavior. There are also implications for program development and intervention with majority students.

Helms's (1985) work is extremely valuable to professionals who wish to increase the multicultural awareness of majority students. For many majority students, the collegiate setting is the first time they really encounter individuals who are racially and culturally different. This creates a special challenge for the development of programs, policies, and services. Helms's theory assists in understanding the approach/avoidance behavior that is often exhibited when multicultural programming is provided. Further, it aids in understanding that the individual progress of students varies and that issues take a great deal of time to work through. Her conceptual framework supports the notion of providing a variety of approaches to increasing multicultural awareness in order to assist students at different developmental stages. Finally, it supports the need for clear and unambiguous behavioral standards that support civility in the campus community. Additional examples could be given for each of the theoretical perspectives described in this volume. Each has a great deal of power to influence practice.

The Translation Process. Several issues are central to the process of translating theory to practice. First, it is essential that student affairs professionals remain current on new theoretical developments. Lack of such knowledge disadvantages our students and ultimately our institutions. Second, we need to know the characteristics of the students whom we serve. Assumptions about student characteristics are usually faulty and careful attention to characteristics such as age, gender, ethnicity, residence, and academic major helps us connect theory to students on our campus. Third, we need to be conscientious about applying theory as we plan new programs or evaluate existing ones. Even just asking the question of what theory tells us about a particular situation and a particular population often provides important insights. Fourth, we need to share what we know about students with students. As practitioners go about the business of training student paraprofessionals or student leaders, presentation of a theoretical perspective is often useful and helpful. Finally, we need to be good observers of what goes on around us and critically evaluate what fits and what does not. New patterns may emerge that need clarification. We are all theory builders, each in our own way.

In the rest of this chapter we provide an agenda of seven issues and topics that need to be addressed in the future. These issues are derived from our analyses of where the profession and the infrastructure of theory and research about college student development have been going.

Agenda for the Future

Continue to Clarify What We Mean by Student Development. Unfortunately, the term student development has been used to describe a movement, a theoretical perspective, a role description, and a set of goals. We do not doubt that in one publication or another we have used the term to imply all these meanings, and maybe even others. For some professionals, the term has been a battle cry; for others, it has been a jargon term signifying nothing. We do not want to propose new jargon, but it is essential in future dialogues to clarify our meanings. For us, student development refers to the goals that colleges have for students (Brown, 1989). Our college catalogs propose that colleges and universities want students to become persons who are intellectually alert, skilled in career specialties, ethical citizens, and interpersonally competent. The most important point we are making when we use the term student development in this way is that we view education as involving the whole person and that the process involves an interaction between developing intellectual and interpersonal competence. Student development as a theoretical framework usually refers to developmental theories, such as the cognitive and sociological theories described in this sourcebook. From our perspective (where the term refers to goals that institutions have for students), any theory that helps us understand how we can help students achieve these developmental and behavioral goals could also be considered a student development theory. Thus, person-environment theories and organizational development theories could be considered student development theories.

Semantics is not one of our favorite games, but when theorists and practitioners line up on different sides of student development as a movement or student development as a theory, and one side is using one meaning and the other side a different meaning, a true dialogue becomes difficult and new professionals become confused. Professionals might freely debate whether or not total student development is an appropriate goal for students (though for us, there is no debate), and they might also deliberate on the relative importance of the developmental educator or the administrator role in student personnel training programs. And we hope that professionals continue to conduct research and debate which theory is most descriptive and relevant. But the adversaries must be clear as to whether they are talking about goals, roles, theories, or movements.

Eliminate the Distinction Between Theorists and Practitioners as a Way of Thinking About Our Roles or Expertise. Nearly a quarter-century ago, Berdie (1966) proposed the scientist-practitioner model for student affairs professionals. Today, too often, we still put each other into categories as "theorists" or "practitioners." It becomes a we-they dialogue. Instead, we need theorists who understand the day-to-day activities and needs of the practitioners, and we need practitioners who approach their day-to-day activities from a solid base of theory and research. Neither professional is complete without the other.

Student Affairs Professionals Must Avoid Intellectual Fads. Fads are a part of intellectual life, as well as what TV programs we watch and what cars we drive. This is true whether we are physicists or educational theorists. The developmental theories used by student affairs professionals are no exception. Thus, the theories proposed by Chickering (1969), Kohlberg (1971), Perry (1970), and Gilligan (1982), for example, have at various times held our attention. The blessing of these theories (and most good theories for that matter) is that they make good intuitive sense and the leap to their practical application is not over too wide a chasm. But student affairs professionals too often either accept or reject new theories uncritically. Few attempts are made to relate the developmental theories to each other, and occasionally other theories about behavior change (for example, person-environment theories) are viewed incorrectly as antithetical to developmental approaches. Also, other developmental domains (for example, the strides made over the past decade in cognitive development) and other developmental theorists (for example, Kegan, 1982) are ignored. This is an unfortunate circumstance since new professionals enter the field with promising abilities but without strong theoretical foundations and too easily succumb to the newest intellectual fad.

Uncritical acceptance of new theories is typical of a professional field in its infancy. Too little research has been done to verify assumptions, which today's professionals too often take for granted (White and Hood, 1989). We hope that as the profession matures new professionals will have the knowledge and expertise to enable them to assess new theories and integrate new ideas without blindly embracing the latest fad.

Explore Ways to Integrate Theories. Having multiple theories of development that provide multiple perspectives on reality is one of the themes of this sourcebook. We believe this theme truly reflects where the profession and the theory and research base are presently situated in understanding college student development. Trying to apply the current theories and models, which have often been derived from studies of white males, to the variety of today's college student subpopulations is inappropriate. Discovering different nuances and variations, as attempts are made to see how current theories do and do not apply to particular student subgroups, is exciting and needs continuous support.

As we discover new ways to look at the development of different student subgroups, however, we must at the same time be looking at the relationships between theories—the commonalities as well as the differences. What this sourcebook presents is a patchwork quilt that encompasses explanations about most student populations and provides frameworks usable by student affairs professionals. This quilt makes it possible for us to consider the subpopulations that interest us the most and point to our theoretical patch as we apply the theory. We can also step back and see that we are part of something larger, the student affairs profession. Each patch contributes to keeping us warm during intellectual winters. Soon, however, we must consider how these patches might be more closely interwoven. We may never have one overarching theory, but having coherently interconnected theories will help us better understand college student life and development. We need to encourage those who attempt the bold and risky venture of synthesizing and integrating the theories. We must continue to strive to understand how students are alike at the same time we discover how they are different from each other.

Determine the Appropriate Balance Between Integration and Differentiation as Developmental Goals. The core of our political society rests on independence and individualism. Though mutual understanding and productive interdependence are espoused as major developmental goals by several theorists, most of our practice focuses on the personal growth of the individual student. Other societies provide greater support to group efforts and interdependence than we do in ours. Our student development theories and their application on the college campus reflect this orientation as we strive to understand how the individual student can be differentiated from the group and establish an individual identity rather than how the student can be integrated into the group and establish a group identity. Our society and our campus culture put substantial effort into searching for ways to help the maturing individual cope with the transitions of leaving community ties (for example, parents, colleagues, spouses, and children) and find new friends, new colleagues, and even a new spouse. Where and when do we provide support for the establishment and maintenance of long-term community relationships? As our student bodies become more diverse in their cultural heritage, our profession needs to examine carefully the relative weight we give to fostering individualism versus community development. The choice is not necessarily either-or, but questions of balance, sequence, and priorities need to be examined. Ultimately, these are basic philosophical questions, though research may provide helpful data when the professional makes decisions.

Research and Evaluation Efforts Must Be Expanded. More research is needed to help us better understand how the college experience can and does influence college students. As theories are proposed and refined, they need to be quickly tested in practice. We suggest that scientists-practitioners refine the theories and evaluate programmatic efforts to apply them in close sequence, if not as parallel efforts. Research needs to be improved in overall quality; it needs to move beyond the ubiquitous survey into more naturalistic studies as well as well-controlled experimental studies. More work is also needed on the design of instruments and indicators of student growth (White and Hood, 1989), and additional emphasis must be given to studies contrasting the development of college students with their age cohorts who do not attend college.

Student Affairs Professionals Must Ask Questions About Who Sets Goals for Students and How Much Intervention Is Appropriate. Student development theories typically use scalar evaluations such as hierarchies (for example, stage 4 is presumably better than stage 3) and the accomplishment of certain skills (for example, maintaining an independent checking account). Even the most process-oriented models suggest that one way of being is probably better than another way of being. Aside from the fact that these are value statements in and of themselves, it is essential to recognize that the goals we have for students, no matter what our theoretical perspective, are value-laden goals that no amount of theorizing or investigative research can prioritize for us. Determining what these goals are and who should set them is a basic question that has not been asked enough by student affairs professionals. We have assumed in the past, for example, that instrumental autonomy and emotional independence are important goals for all students. Now we recognize that not all cultures accept these as high-priority goals.

Higher education has nearly succumbed to a redefinition of the successful student, from that of being an educated person, true scholar, and good citizen, to being the student with the highest grade point average and maximum career moxie. What does developmental theory say about our definitions of success? What does our philosophy of life have to tell us about what is the good life? Is it appropriate for us to intervene and try to influence what goals students choose, as well as how they may reach their goals? These questions have been asked for centuries, and we must continue to debate them.

Conclusion

There are barriers that must be overcome if theory is to become a useful tool for student affairs professionals. Too often, however, we make the task of translating theory to practice much more complex than necessary. The issues raised here are highly interrelated. The goals we have for students, for example, are derived from philosophical beliefs about their importance in our society. But what goals we give priority to has practical implications, and how we seek to bring about student change is influenced by psychological or organizational theory and research findings. We believe the seven agenda items discussed above are only a beginning. Each item could be expanded with its own detailed agenda, and undoubtedly other items can be added. Not every professional can work on all the items, but we hope that each reader finds at least one agenda item that is sufficiently stimulating or provocative to motivate self-inquiry and hence self-improvement. There is much work to be done if our institutional goals of promoting college student development are to be reached with maximum benefits for our students.

References

Berdie, R. F. "Student Personnel Work: Definition and Redefinition." *Journal of College Student Personnel,* 1966, *7,* 131–136.

Brown, R. D. *Student Development in Today's Higher Education: A Return to the Academy.* Student Personnel Monograph, no. 16. Washington, D.C.: American College Personnel Association, 1972.

Brown, R. D. "Fostering Intellectual and Personal Growth: The Student Development Role." In U. Delworth, G. Hanson, and Associates (eds.), *Student Services: A Handbook for the Profession.* (2nd ed.) San Francisco: Jossey-Bass, 1989.

Chickering, A. W. *Education and Identity.* San Francisco: Jossey-Bass, 1969.

Cross, W. E., Jr. "Black Family and Black Identity: A Literature Review." *Western Journal of Black Studies,* 1978, *2,* 111–124.

Gilligan, C. *In a Different Voice.* Cambridge, Mass.: Harvard University Press, 1982.

Helms, J. E. "Cultural Identity in the Treatment Process." In P. Pederson (ed.), *Handbook of Cross-Cultural Counseling and Therapy.* Westport, Conn.: Greenwood Press, 1985.

Hoy, W., and Miskel, C. (eds.). *Educational Administration: Theory, Research, and Practice.* New York: Random House, 1978.

Hurst, J., and Jacobson, J. "Theories Underlying Students' Needs for Programs." In M. J. Barr, L. A. Keating, and Associates (eds.), *Developing Effective Student Services Programs: Systematic Approaches for Practitioners.* San Francisco: Jossey-Bass, 1985.

Kegan, R. *The Evolving Self: Problems and Process in Human Development.* Cambridge, Mass.: Harvard University Press, 1982.

Kohlberg, L. "Stages of Moral Development." In C. M. Beck, B. S. Crittenden, and E. V. Sullivan (eds.), *Moral Education.* Toronto: University of Toronto Press, 1971.

Perry, W. G. *Forms of Intellectual and Ethical Development in College.* New York: Holt, Rinehart & Winston, 1970.

Sanford, N. (ed.). *The American College.* New York: Wiley, 1962.

White, D. B., and Hood, A. B. "An Assessment of the Validity of Chickering's Theory of Student Development." *Journal of College Student Development,* 1989, *30* (4), 354–362.

Winston, R. B., Jr., and Miller, T. K. *Developmental Task and Lifestyle Inventory Manual.* Athens, Ga.: Student Development Associates, 1987.

Robert D. Brown is Carl A. Happold Distinguished Professor of educational psychology at the University of Nebraska, Lincoln. He is past president of the American College Personnel Association and past editor of the Journal of College Student Development.

Margaret J. Barr is vice-chancellor for student affairs at Texas Christian University, Fort Worth. She is a past president of the American College Personnel Association and in 1985 received the NASPA Contribution to Literature and Research Award and the ACPA Professional Service Award.

APPENDIX: ADDITIONAL RESOURCES

Theories and Models About Personal Growth and Development

This cluster of theories has been presented in Chapter One. Practitioners who wish to update their knowledge in this area may refer to the works of Brown, Chickering, Erikson, Heath, Holland, Loevinger, Rogers, Sanford, and Super. The most recent addition to this cluster is the work of Fowler. Although the stages of faith were published in the mid 1970s, student affairs practitioners have just recently incorporated faith development into their goals for student growth. In addition to reading the explanation of faith development found in Chapter One, the reader may wish to review the following source:

Fowler, J. "Stages of Faith: The Structured Developmental Approach." In T. C. Hennessey (ed.), *Values and Moral Development.* New York: Paulist Press, 1976.

Theories and Models About the Way We Think and Make Meaning

This group of theories is reviewed in Chapters One, Two, and Three. The works of Belenky and others, Gilligan, King, Kitchener, Kohlberg, Kolb, Perry, and Piaget form the base for this cluster. In addition to the sources cited in the References of the first three chapters, two other sources are recommended:

Kitchener, K. S. "Intuition, Critical Evaluation, and Ethical Principles: The Foundation for Ethical Decisions in Counseling Psychology." *Counseling Psychologist,* 1984, *12,* 43–55.

Rest, J. R. *Moral Development: Advances in Research and Theory.* New York: Praeger, 1986.

Theories About the Process of Growing and Changing

This cluster is emerging as one of the newest perspectives for understanding growth and change as a special process rather than as a different phenomenon included but not explained in each developmental theory. Gilligan, Gould, and Schlossberg are particularly important contributors to this perspective on growth and change. Chapter Three includes a good overview of growth and change as defined from this new perspective.

Theories and Models About Campus Environments

As mentioned in the Editor's Notes, space limitations resulted in a cursory treatment of campus environments in this volume. Included here are some additional references to supplement the discussion in Chapter Six.

Banning, J. H. (ed.). *Campus Ecology: A Perspective for Student Affairs.* Cincinnati, Ohio: National Association of Student Personnel Administrators, 1978.

Banning, J. H., and McKinley, D. L. "Conceptions of the Campus Environment." In W. H. Morrill and J. C. Hurst (eds.), *Dimensions of Intervention for Student Development.* New York: Wiley, 1980.

Moos, R. H. *Evaluating Educational Environments: Procedures, Measures, Findings, and Policy Implications.* San Francisco: Jossey-Bass, 1979.

Theories and Models About Student Populations

Clearly, this area has expanded the most rapidly. Chapters Two, Three, Four, and Five are devoted to discussions of various subpopulations and models and theories about them. Other sources that have contributed significantly to our understanding of various student populations are the following:

Baker, F. M. "The Afro-American Life Cycle: Success, Failure, and Mental Health." *Journal of the National Medical Association,* 1987, *79,* 625–633.

Baldwin, J. A., and Bell, Y. R. "The African Self-Consciousness Scale: An Africentric Personality Questionnaire." *Western Journal of Black Studies,* 1985, 9, 61–68.

Brown, J. E. *The Spiritual Legacy of the American Indian.* New York: Crossroad, 1987.

Cooley, C. R. "Cultural Effects on Indian Education: An Application of Social Learning Theory." *Journal of American Indian Education,* 1977, *17,* 21–27.

Fleming, J. *Blacks in College: A Comparative Study of Students' Success in Black and in White Institutions.* San Francisco: Jossey-Bass, 1984.

Gibbs, J. T. "Patterns of Adaptation Among Black Students at a Predominantly White University: Selected Case Studies." *American Journal of Orthopsychiatry,* 1974, *44,* 728–740.

Hill, R. B. "Economic Forces, Structural Discrimination, and Black Families' Instability." In H. E. Cheatham and J. B. Stewart (eds.), *Black Families: Interdisciplinary Perspectives.* New Brunswick, N.J.: Rutgers University Press, 1989.

Jackson, G. "Conceptualizing Afrocentric and Eurocentric Mental Health Training." In H. P. Lefley and P. Pedersen (eds.), *Cross-Cultural Training for Mental Health Professions.* Springfield, Ill.: Thomas, 1986.

Leong, F.T.L. "Counseling and Psychotherapy with Asian-Americans: A Review of the Literature." *Journal of Counseling Psychology,* 1986, 33, 196–206.

Name Index

SUBJECT INDEX

Ordering Information

New Directions for Student Services is a series of paperback books that offers guidelines and programs for aiding students in their total development—emotional, social, and physical, as well as intellectual. Books in the series are published quarterly in Fall, Winter, Spring, and Summer and are available for purchase by subscription as well as by single copy.

Subscriptions for 1990 cost $42.00 for individuals (a savings of 20 percent over single-copy prices) and $56.00 for institutions, agencies, and libraries. Please do not send institutional checks for personal subscriptions. Standing orders are accepted.

Single copies cost $12.95 when payment accompanies order. (California, New Jersey, New York, and Washington, D.C., residents please include appropriate sales tax.) Billed orders will be charged postage and handling.

Discounts for quantity orders are available. Please write to the address below for information.

All orders must include either the name of an individual or an official purchase order number. Please submit your order as follows:

Subscriptions: specify series and year subscription is to begin
Single copies: include individual title code (such as SS1)

Mail all orders to:
Jossey-Bass Inc., Publishers
350 Sansome Street
San Francisco, California 94104

OTHER TITLES AVAILABLE IN THE NEW DIRECTIONS FOR STUDENT SERVICES SERIES

Margaret J. Barr, Editor-in-Chief; *M. Lee Upcraft*, Associate Editor

SS50 Community Service as Values Education, *Cecilia I. Delve, Suzanné D. Mintz, Greig M. Stewart*
SS49 Crisis Intervention and Prevention, *Harold L. Pruett, Vivian B. Brown*
SS48 Designing Campus Activities to Foster a Sense of Community, *Dennis C. Roberts*
SS47 Responding to Violence on Campus, *Jan M. Sherrill, Dorothy G. Siegel*
SS46 Religion on Campus, *John Butler*
SS45 Dealing with the Behavioral and Psychological Problems of Students, *Ursula Delworth*
SS44 Empowering Women: Leadership Development Strategies on Campus, *Mary Ann Danowitz Sagaria*
SS43 Performance Appraisal as a Tool for Staff Development, *Robert D. Brown*
SS42 Changing Roles for Men on Campus, *Ronald J. May, Murray Scher*
SS41 Managing Student Affairs Effectively, *M. Lee Upcraft, Margaret J. Barr*
SS40 Fraternities and Sororities on the Contemporary College Campus, *Roger B. Winston, Jr., William R. Nettles III, John H. Opper, Jr.*
SS39 Enhancing Campus Judicial Systems, *Robert Caruso, Will W. Travelstead*
SS38 Responding to the Needs of Today's Minority Students, *Doris J. Wright*
SS37 Expanding Opportunities for Professional Education, *Leila V. Moore, Robert B. Young*
SS36 Guiding the Development of Foreign Students, *K Richard Pyle*
SS35 Alcohol and the College Student, *Thomas G. Goodale*
SS34 Developing Campus Recreation and Wellness Programs, *Fred Leafgren*
SS33 Enhancing Relationships with the Student Press, *John H. Schuh*
SS32 Working with the Parents of College Students, *Robert D. Cohen*
SS31 Coping with Death on Campus, *Ellen S. Zinner*
SS30 Applied Ethics in Student Services, *Harry J. Canon, Robert D. Brown*
SS29 Facilitating the Development of Women, *Nancy J. Evans*
SS28 Rethinking Services for College Athletes, *Arthur Shriberg, Frederick R. Brodzinski*
SS27 Students as Paraprofessional Staff, *Steven C. Ender, Roger B. Winston, Jr.*
SS26 Enhancing Student Development with Computers, *Cynthia S. Johnson, K Richard Pyle*
SS25 Orienting Students to College, *M. Lee Upcraft*
SS24 Commuter Students: Enhancing Their Educational Experiences, *Sylvia S. Stewart*
SS23 Understanding Student Affairs Organizations, *George D. Kuh*
SS22 Student Affairs and the Law, *Margaret J. Barr*
SS21 Helping Students Manage Stress, *Elizabeth M. Altmaier*
SS20 Measuring Student Development, *Gary R. Hanson*
SS19 Mentoring-Transcript Systems for Promoting Student Growth, *Robert D. Brown, David A. DeCoster*
SS17 Developmental Approaches to Academic Advising, *Roger B. Winston, Jr., Steven C. Ender, Theodore K. Miller*
SS16 Understanding Today's Students, *David DeCoster, Phyllis Mable*
SS15 Education for Student Development, *Jane Fried*
SS14 Facilitating Students' Career Development, *Vincent A. Harren, M. Harry Daniels, Jacqueline N. Buch*
SS10 Serving Handicapped Students, *Hazel Z. Sprandel, Marlin R. Schmidt*
SS6 Utilizing Futures Research, *Frederick R. Brodzinski*
SS5 Consulting on Campus, *M. Kathryn Hamilton, Charles J. Meade*
SS4 Applying New Developmental Findings, *Lee Knefelkamp, Carole Widick, Clyde A. Parker*